DATE DUE			
	WITHDRAWN		
Highline College Library			

DIMENSIONAL ILLUSTRATORS, INC. SOUTHAMPTON, PENNSYLVANIA

2

ROCKPORT PUBLISHERS ROCKPORT, MASSACHUSETTS

DISTRIBUTED BY NORTH LIGHT BOOKS, CINCINNATI, OHIO

3-DIMENSIONAL ILLUSTRATION

Winners

Of The

First Annual

Dimensional

Illustrators

Awards

Show

Produced by Dimensional Illustrators, Inc.
Southampton, Pennsylvania

Published by Rockport Publishers, Inc.,
Five Smith Street
Rockport, Massachusetts 01966

Distributed to the book trade and art trade in the U.S.
and Canada by:
North Light, an imprint of Writer's Digest Books
1507 Dana Avenue
Cincinnati, Ohio 45207
Telephone: (513) 531-2222

Distributed to the book trade and art trade
throughout the rest of the world by:
Hearst Books International
105 Madison Avenue (20th floor)
New York, New York 10016
Telephone: (212) 481-0355

Other Distribution by:
Rockport, Publishers, Inc.
Five Smith Street
Rockport, Massachusetts 01966
Telephone: (508) 546-9590
Fax: (508) 546-7141
Easy Link: 62945477

Address Direct Mail Sales to:

Nick Greco
Dimensional Illustrators, Inc.
362 Second Street Pike, Suite 112
Southampton, Pennsylvania 18966
Telephone: (215) 953-1415
Fax: (215) 953-1697

Library of Congress-in-Publication Data

3-DIMENSIONAL ILLUSTRATION
THE BEST IN 3-D ADVERTISING AND PUBLISHING WORLDWIDE

EXECUTIVE EDITOR
Nick Greco
Dimensional Illustrators, Inc.

CREATIVE DIRECTOR
Kathleen Ziegler
Dimensional Illustrators, Inc.

DESIGNER
Scott M. Fixari
Hill Design Group, Inc.

THANKS
For their dedication and expertise:
Deborah Davis
Magge McCann
Sharon Newman

SPECIAL THANKS
For their encouragement and support:
Ann and Bob Ziegler

COVER PHOTOGRAPH
Pohlman Studios, Inc.

COVER ILLUSTRATION
Joan Kritchman Knuteson
Advertising Art Studios, Inc.
710 North Plankinton Avenue
Milwaukee, Wisconsin 53203-2454
Telephone: (414) 276-6306

PHOTOGRAPHY
p. 6   Underwater Scene
        Kathleen Ziegler
p. 10   DNA Model
        Andrew Eccles
p. 10   World Model
        Kathleen Ziegler
p. 246 World Model
        Kathleen Ziegler

"Dimensional Illustration, when combined with an original concept, has an attraction and special effect that would be nearly impossible to achieve with 2-Dimensional work-either photographically or in illustration."

JOAN KRITCHMAN KNUTESON

Joan is an accomplished 3-Dimensional illustrator working in paper sculpture and mixed media. She works in papers, model paste, wood and assemblage of found objects. The "Paper Tiger" sculpture was created to reinforce a campaign for a Micro film machine which printed on bond paper. Joan's awards include, Print Regional Design Annual, Studio Magazine Award Annual-Merit for Illustration, BPAA Awards-Best of Division-Illustration and Excellence Awards-Illustration, and the First Dimensional Illustrators Awards Show-Gold and Silver awards.

NEW DIMENSIONS IN ILLUSTRATION
FIRST ANNUAL DIMENSIONAL ILLUSTRATORS AWARDS SHOW

CLAY, PLASTIC, PAPER SCULPTURE / WOOD / FABRIC / COLLAGE / 3-D ASSEMBLAGE / MIXED MEDIA

CONTENTS

Paper Collage
Julia Davis Age 5

Clay Sculpture
Catie Davis Age 9

8

As children in school, many of our initial creative experiences involve the use of dimensional mediums such as clay, cut paper construction and mixed media assemblages. Since the world is viewed in three-dimension, dimensional illustration becomes a natural creative process. Today's talented illustrators couple the intuitive experiences of youth with the sophisticated techniques of modern modelmakers to create provocative three-dimensional illustrations. The Dimensional Illustrators Awards Show and Exhibition is dedicated to showcasing the burgeoning industry of 3-Dimensional illustration.

With the use of 3-Dimensional illustration there arises an entirely different set of demands on the art director, client and modelmaker. The illustrator must be skilled in sculptural techniques, dimensional perspective and photography. The diversification of this unique hybrid medium captures the attention of the viewer while prolonging the reality of the illustration. The end result being a *trompe l'oeil* without the brush strokes.

Today's creative professionals are using 3-Dimensional illustration as a visually stimulating adjunct to the advertising and publishing industry. The impact in the print media is apparent in the award winning entries presented in *3-Dimensional Illustration-The Best In 3-D Advertising And Publishing Worldwide.* The First Annual Dimensional Illustrators Awards Show is an international competition which identifies the artistic medium of 3-Dimensional illustrators while applauding the achievements of those imaginative art directors responsible for choosing a 3-Dimensional solution.

I would like to extend my personal thanks and congratulations to the award winners for promoting the genre of 3-Dimensional Illustration and encourage you to continue your efforts to awaken the consciousness of the visual communications community to the realities of this most singular dynamic industry.

KATHLEEN ZIEGLER
PRESIDENT
DIMENSIONAL ILLUSTRATORS, INC.

World Model Mixed Media
Kathleen Ziegler

DNA Plastic Sculpture
Kathleen Ziegler

As we enter the 1990's, it has become apparent that a welcome plethora of 3-Dimensional illustrations are providing an oasis of innovative solutions for the advertising and publishing industry. Today's art directors are embracing the challenges of 3-Dimensional design with renewed enthusiasm. Many creative professionals, sensitive to the demands of a sophisticated consumer, are using 3-Dimensional models as an essential ingredient of their creative concepts. I applaud the imaginative art directors whose innovative use of three-dimensional illustration has placed them in the vanguard of the visual communications industry. Your contributions to the advertising and publishing industry will long be recognized for their ingenious application of 3-Dimensional illustration.

NICK GRECO
VICE PRESIDENT
DIMENSIONAL ILLUSTRATORS, INC.

NANCY ALDRICH-RUENZEL

Nancy is currently the Editorial Director of *Step-By-Step Graphics* magazine, the how-to reference magazine for professional visual communicators working in all graphic disciplines including 3-Dimensional design. As Vice President of *Step-By-Step Publishing,* she also oversees the development of Step-By-Step books, as well as the how-to publication geared specifically to graphic designers and illustrators working on the desktop, called *Step-By-Step Electronic Design.* She received her Master of Arts from Indiana University and her Bachelor of Arts from the University of Wisconsin-Madison.

She is a seasoned practitioner who has worn many hats in a variety of areas within the graphic arts and publishing fields in the past ten years. She is a lecturer, and serves on the board of GRAFIX, the National Conference for Graphic Design Professionals. She is also a member of the American Institute of Graphic Arts, and the American Center for Design. Under Nancy's editorial leadership, *Step-By-Step Graphics* and *Step-By-Step Electronic Design,* have won numerous awards.

PATRICK J. CREAVEN

Pat is currently Senior VP Group Head Art Director at William Douglas McAdams Inc., New York City. He attended Arizona State and is a graduate of Pratt Institute. He has also held art and designer positions at Merck, Sharp & Dohme International and Grey Advertising.

Pat has won numerous pharmaceutical industry awards including the Aesculapius Award, Silver Metal RX Club Show, New York Art Directors Club, New York Advertising Club Gold Metal, New York International Advertising Festival, Desi and AIGA Awards, as well as the 1989 First Annual Dimensional Illustrators Awards Show.

LOU DIJOSEPH

Lou is currently Executive Vice President Creative Director of Young & Rubicam, New York City. He was born in Philadelphia and is a graduate of The University of the Arts, majoring in advertising design. Lou served with the US Army as Lieutenant, Infantry. During his tenure at Young & Rubicam, he has served as Art Supervisor to Senior VP Associate Creative Director, as well as Executive Creative Director. He is a past president of Bianchi Films, and has served as a Freelance Creative Consultant, Writer and TV Producer. From 1979-81, Lou was Senior VP, Group Creative Director, US Army Recruitment Account, with the firm of N.W. Ayer.

As Creative Director at Young & Rubicam his clients included, Adidas, AT&T, Dr Pepper, General Foods, Gillette, and the US Army. Lou was awarded the AD Club Gold award for his Dr Pepper campaign, *America's Most Misunderstood Softdrink* and AD Club Silver award for, *The Most Original Soft Drink Ever.* In 1980, he won the Clio award, Andy Merit award and One Show Merit award. He was a Kelly award finalist in 1981 for, *Be All You Can Be,* U.S. Army. Lou is a recipient of the Distinguished Civilian Service Medal from the US Army and Clio award for art direction of the Dr Pepper campaigns in 1985 and 1986.

THE JUDGING FOR THE FIRST ANNUAL DIMENSION-
AL ILLUSTRATORS AWARDS SHOW AND EXHIBITION
WAS HELD AT THE ART DIRECTORS CLUB OF NEW
YORK. THE QUALITY AND SUCCESS OF AN AWARDS
SHOW LIES IN THE INTEGRITY, EXPERTISE AND PRO-
FESSIONALISM OF THE JURORS. AS OUTSTANDING
REPRESENTATIVES OF THE ADVERTISING AND
PUBLISHING INDUSTRY, OUR JUDGES HAVE
CHOSEN THE BEST IN 3-DIMENSIONAL ILLUSTRA-
TION WORLDWIDE. THE 400 AWARD WINNERS
SELECTED FOR THE EXHIBITION HAVE ENGENDERED
A RENEWED AWARENESS OF 3-DIMENSIONAL IL-
LUSTRATION IN TODAY'S CREATIVE COMMUNITY.
DIMENSIONAL ILLUSTRATORS, INC. WISHES TO
THANK THE JUDGES FOR THEIR CONTRIBUTION TO
THIS MOST SINGULAR INDUSTRY, AND WE HOPE
THAT THEY WILL CONTINUE TO ABOUND IN
CREATIVE ENDEAVORS.

DAVID EPSTEIN

David is an internationally known Graphic Designer, 3-Dimensional Illustrator, Author and Educator. He is a Professor of Graphic and Packaging Design at Pratt Institute in Brooklyn, New York. David is a graduate of the Cooper Union Art School and has long been active in its alumni affairs. His articles and works have appeared in *Graphis Magazine, Graphis Annuals, CA Magazine, Print Magazine, Art Direction Magazine* and *Illustration In The Third Dimension*.

David has served on the New York Art Directors Club Executive Board for three terms and has been honored with over 70 major awards and exhibitions, including a one man retrospective of his 3-Dimensional work. Some of his clients include, The Upjohn Company, The New York Times, Allied Chemical, Volkswagen of America, Consumer Reports and Redbook Magazine.

He has conducted nationally acclaimed seminars in advanced graphic design and is a contributing editor of *Step-By-Step Graphics*. He is the author of many articles on 3-Dimensional Illustration, graphics and packaging design.

ELAINE GOLAK

Elaine received her Bachelor of Fine Arts degree from Moore College of Art in Philadelphia. After several years in the advertising industry, Elaine is currently concentrating her efforts on her own visual merchandising firm in Bristol, Pennsylvania. As a freelance fabric design artist, she has worked in 3-Dimensional window interiors and design for many of the top firms in Philadelphia, including J.E. Caldwell, Strawbridge & Clothier and the US Army. As a master craftswoman in the fabric arts, Elaine has created numerous fabric sculptures and designs placing her among an elite group of display designers in the United States.

MEREDITH HAMILTON

Meredith is currently the Associate Art Director, Graphics for *Newsweek* magazine. She directs a five-person department that produces information graphics, as well as diagrams, maps and charts for all editions of the magazine. She works closely with section editors and page designers to ensure that graphics are pertinent and allocated proper space. From 1985-87, Meredith was the Assistant Art Director for *Discover Magazine*, where she worked exclusively on diagrams and illustrations, did research, and produced detailed sketches of concepts. She holds a Comparative Literature A.B. with Honors from Brown University and is a graduate of Parson's School of Design, Department of Illustration, Dean's List. She is also a successful freelance illustrator.

Peter began his career at FCB England, as a Creative Director. While working at FCB, he was responsible for work on Dulux paints, Cadbury, British Airways and London Transport. He moved to Grey in 1984 to work on Mary Quant Cosmetics, Mercedes-Benz automobiles, Nike footwear, Beecham Resolve and Tennent's Extra Lager. Peter has won many major UK and international awards across virtually all of his accounts. One of his best known ads -Fly The Tube- has been exhibited in the New York Museum of Modern Art.

Jake is currently the Director of Creative Services for the Chilton Company in Radnor, Pennsylvania. He is a graduate of Penn State University and The University of the Arts. From 1979-89, he served as Design Director of Magazines for Springhouse Corporation and has worked for numerous agencies and design firms including, Kap Studios, Studio Three and Hallmark Cards.

Jake is a past member of the Board of Directors of the Philadelphia Art Directors Club and the Hussian School of Art. During his admirable career he has won numerous awards from the Philadelphia Art Directors Club, Society of Publication Designers, Type Directors Club, Folio 400 and the 1989 Dimensional Illustrators Awards Show.

Will Vinton, founder of Will Vinton Productions in Portland, Oregon is the creator of the clay animation process trademarked Claymation.® Mr Vinton is recognized as the foremost authority on clay animation in the world. He worked for several years as a producer, photographer, sound technician and editor on productions ranging from television commercials and industrial documentaries to live-action shorts and features.

Beginning with an Academy Award in 1975 for best Animated Short Film for *Closed Mondays*, co-created with Bob Gardiner, Mr. Vinton has since garnered Oscar nominations for *Rip Van Winkle*, *The Creation*, *The Great Cognito* and *Return to Oz*. The studio's television achievements include two Emmy Awards for *Claymation Christmas Celebration* and a live action Claymation sequence of *Moonlighting*. The television special Meet the Raisins received an Emmy nomination.

In 1986 Will Vinton Productions created the most memorable television commercial of all time, *The California Raisins*™, for the California Raisin Advisory Board. Other commercial clients include, Domino's Pizza, General Foods, Frito Lay, Levi's Jeans, Nike and Seven Eleven. The commercial division has received the advertising Clio Award for Scotsman Publications and *The California Raisins*.

PAPER SCULPTURE

THE BASIC PAPER SCULPTURE TECHNIQUES OF SCORING, CURLING AND FOLDING ARE USED TO TRANSFORM PAPER INTO A STRUCTURALLY COMPLEX COMPOSITION. THIS RIGID BUT PLIABLE MEDIUM AFFORDS THE DISCIPLINED DIMENSIONAL ILLUSTRATORS A VARIETY OF INTRINSICALLY DISTINCTIVE IMAGES. WHEN PHOTOGRAPHED, THE PRISTINE QUALITY OF THE PAPER IS AESTHETICALLY ENHANCED BY THE VISUAL ILLUSION OF LIGHT AND SHADOW THEREBY ADDING GREATER DIMENSIONAL PERSPECTIVE TO THE OVERALL ILLUSTRATION.

P A P E R
S C U L P T U R E

"I call 3-Dimensional illustration extended reality. The print media is a world of 2-Dimensional images. The images come and go as you turn the page. But with a 3-Dimensional illustration, your mind immediately lingers, aware that the image had to have existed in some prior place, at some prior time. Your response to the printed page is extended by your awareness. In the intense, competitive world of advertising and publishing, that extra micro-moment of attention from the reader, that lingering wonderment, can make an enormous difference."

D A V I D   E P S T E I N

Dimensional
Illustrator: *Soren Thaae*
Art Director: *Jan Hovman*
Photographer: *Svend Lindbaek*
Agency: *Createam*
Client: *Baltica Insurance Company*
Category: *Advertising Direct Mail Poster*

Dimensional
Illustrator: *Joan Kritchman Knuteson*
Art Director: *Bob Hillmer*
Photographer: *Charles Ruggles*
Agency: *Communitec*
Client: *Micro Design*
Category: *Calendar*

Dimensional
Illustrator: *Bill Finewood*
Art Director: *Jennifer St.Denis*
Photographer: *Bill Finewood*
Agency: *Art Works, Inc.*
Publisher: *Sunrise Publications*
Category: *Editorial Illustration*

Dimensional
Illustrator: *Bill Miller*
Art Director: *Bill Miller*
Photographer: *Bill Miller*
Agency: *Bill Miller Studio*
Publisher: *Bill Miller*
Client: *Paper Classics*
Category: *Advertising Illustration*

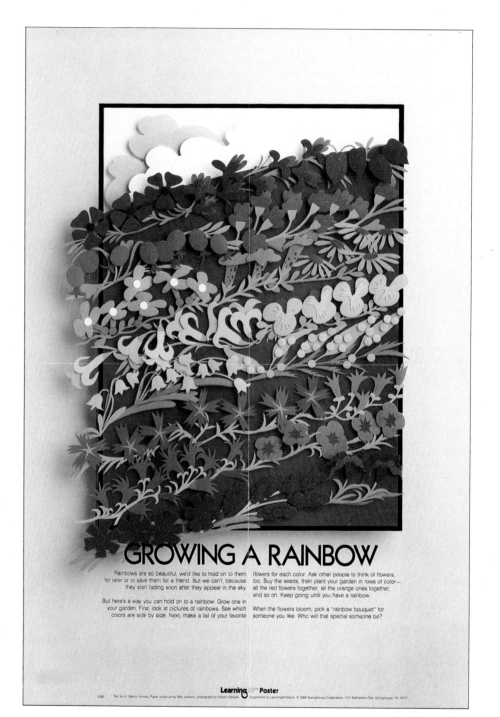

Dimensional
Illustrator: *Bob Jackson*
Art Director: *Dyann Craven*
Photographer: *Robert Hakalski*
Publisher: *Springhouse Corporation*
Client: *Learning '89*
Category: *Advertising Direct Mail Business*

[THE JOYS OF PHYSICIAN HEALTH INSURANCE]

FIRST,
A MEDICAL DEGREE.
THEN,
THE THIRD DEGREE.

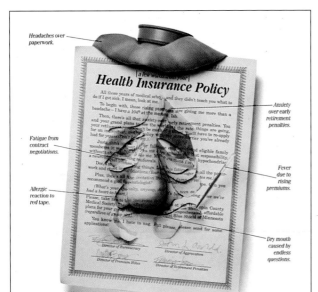

COOL DOWN.

Have a seat.
You may qualify for insurance that's especially formulated to help relieve the common ailments of physician-practice health coverage.

The Hennepin County Medical Society and Blue Cross and Blue Shield of Minnesota are pleased to offer comprehensive, affordable protection to members of organized medicine within Minnesota.

And to their eligible dependents and full-time employees.

However large or small your practice, we can prescribe a full dose of group-level coverage. Without the usual dose of red tape.

We can protect your early retirement benefits.

We can even update you on federal and state benefit laws.

If you're currently *not* covered by Blue Cross and Blue Shield of Minnesota, consider either—or both—of these flexible options, available now through the Hennepin County Medical Society:

AWARE GOLD LIMITED—with a $10 co-payment per office visit.

SILVER SERIES—with an annual deductible of $500, $1000 or $2000.

Optional dental coverage can be prescribed for either plan.

For more information, return the reply card. Or call the Insurance Department at Hennepin County Medical Society, Twin Cities, 623-3030. In-state, 1-800-882-7999.

We'll be right with you.

PRESCRIBE NOW.

Please prescribe _____ application(s) for physician-practice health insurance, one for each person in my group who desires coverage. (Requesting a premium quote binds no one to a policy. Additional information will be sent with the application(s).)

As a member of organized medicine within Minnesota, I belong to:

☐ AMA
☐ MMA
☐ HCMS
OTHER_____

NAME		
GROUP NAME		
OFFICE MANAGER		
ADDRESS		
CITY	STATE	ZIP
PHONE		
SIGNATURE	DATE	

Dimensional
Illustrator: *Tim Nyberg*
Art Directors: *Tim Simmons/Eric Edward Brown*
Photographer: *Anthony Simmons*
Agency: *shoestring advertising/Tim Simmons Design*
Client: *Hennepin County Medical Society*
Category: *Advertising Illustration*
Advertising Direct Mail Business

Dimensional
Illustrator: *Edward S.F. Chan*
Art Directors: *Edward S.F.Chan/Alex Chan/Ron Cheung*
Agency: *Lintas: Hong Kong*
Client: *Centaline Agencies, Ltd.*
Category: *Advertising Magazine Campaign*

Dimensional
Illustrator: *Jeff Nishinaka*
Art Director: *Sven Lindman*
Photographer: *Jeff Nishinaka*
Agency: *Klemtner Advertising*
Publisher: *Medical Trade Publications*
Client: *Wyeth-Ayerst Laboratories*
Category: *Advertising Magazine Business Spread*

Dimensional
Illustrator: *Marilyn Bass*
Photographer: *Marvin Goldman*
Category: *Advertising Illustration*

Dimensional
Illustrator: *Ajin*
Art Director: *Danielle Gallo*
Publisher: *Penthouse Letters*
Category: *Editorial Illustration*

Dimensional
Illustrator: *Olive Alpert*
Art Directors: *Dale Fiorillo/Gerry Counihan*
Photographer: *Jelly Bean*
Publisher: *Dell Publishing*
Client: *Dell Publishing*
Category: *Illustration Editorial*

Dimensional
Illustrator: *Andrew Nitzberg*
Category: *Self Promotion*

SILVER
AWARD

Dimensional
Illustrator: *Joan Kritchman Knuteson*
Photographer: *Charles Ruggles*
Agency: *Advertising Art Studios*
Category: *Unpublished*

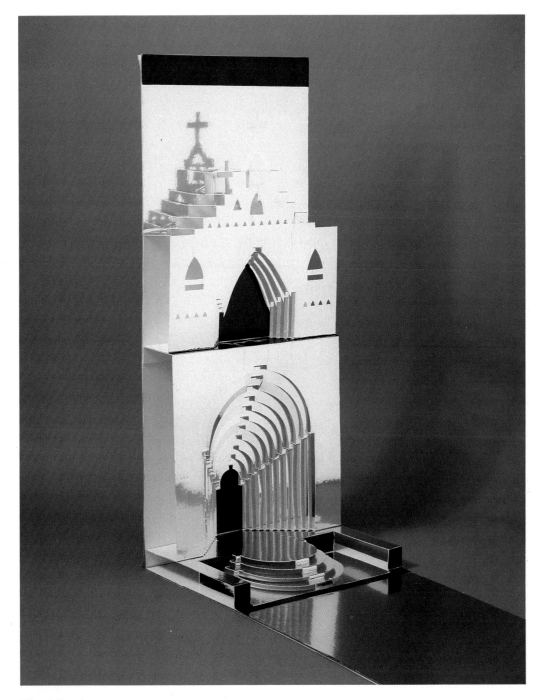

Dimensional
Illustrator: *William Robert Ives*
Art Director: *William Robert Ives*
Photographer: *Bob Grubb & Sons*
Agency: *Ives Designs*
Category: *Greeting Card*

SILVER
AWARD

Dimensional
Illustrator: *Bill Crawford*
Art Director: *Jim Scharnberg*
Agency: *Richman Sales Promotion & Corporate Design*
Client: *Pennsylvania Manufactures Association Insurance*
Category: *Editorial Magazine Business Cover*

Dimensional
Illustrator: *Andrew Nitzberg*
Art Director: *Edward Rosanio*
Publisher: *Springhouse Corporation*
Client: *Nursing '88*
Category: *Magazine Editorial Business Spread*

Dimensional
Illustrator: *Richard McNeel*
Art Director: *Roger Dowd*
Photographer: *Richard McNeel*
Agency: *Medical Economics Company*
Publisher: *Jim Jenkins*
Client: *Medical Economics Magazine*
Category: *Editorial Magazine Business Cover*

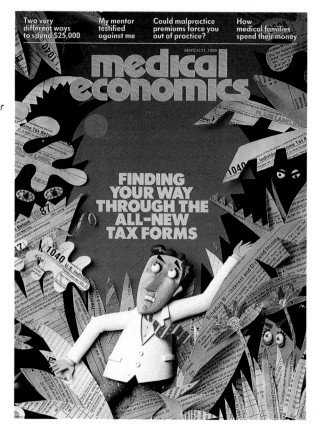

Dimensional
Illustrator: *Andrew Nitzberg*
Art Director: *Darcy Feralio*
Photographer: *Robert Hakawski*
Publisher: *Charles Mitchell*
Client: *Office Systems '88*
Category: *Magazine Editorial Business Spread*

Dimensional
Illustrator: *Susan Ash*
Art Directors: *Greg Kindred/Margaret Seburn*
Photographer: *Steve Hix*
Agency: *Ravenhill Represents*
Publisher: *Veterinary Medicine Publishing Company*
Client: *Veterinary Economics*
Category: *Magazine Editorial Business Cover*

Dimensional
Illustrator: *Andrew Nitzberg*
Art Director: *David Beverage*
Photographer: *Gary Donnelly*
Publisher: *Charles Mitchell*
Client: *Office Systems '89*
Category: *Magazine Editorial Business Spread*

Dimensional
Illustrator: *Jack Graham*
Art Director: *Rand Carlson*
Photographer: *Dave Ragsdale*
Publisher: *Donald V. Dotts*
Client: *ASU Alumni Association*
Category: *Editorial Magazine Business Cover*

Dimensional
Illustrator: *Jerry Pavey*
Art Director: *Jerry Pavey*
Photographer: *Tom Radcliffe*
Agency: *Jerry Pavey Design & Illustration*
Publisher: *Svec/Conway Printing*
Client: *The Sulphur Institute*
Category: *Magazine Editorial Business Cover*

Dimensional
Illustrator: *Bill Crawford*
Art Director: *Peter Stolvoort*
Agency: *Mueller & Wister Inc.*
Publisher: *Communique*
Client: *Wyeth-Ayerst*
Category: *Editorial Magazine Business Cover*

Dimensional
Illustrator: *Bill Crawford*
Art Director: *Peter Stolvoort*
Agency: *Mueller & Wister Inc.*
Publisher: *Communique*
Client: *Wyeth-Ayerst*
Category: *Editorial Magazine Business Spread*

For women, the late 40s and mid-50s bring on a real mid-life crisis, which in some aspects can be psychological, but which is actually precipitated by the physiological changes that occur during menopause.

A woman's endogenous estrogen levels decrease during natural menopause and when a woman undergoes surgical menopause (hysterectomy). Estrogens are needed by the body for the development and maintenance of the female reproductive system. Menopause, however, can hinder the maintenance process by lessening the amount of estrogens in a woman's body.

The decreased hormone levels can also produce vasomotor symptoms, such as "hot flashes," atrophic vaginitis, and related discomforts. Often accompanying these symptoms are associated sweating, insomnia, irritability, and depression. All of these can greatly disrupt a woman's lifestyle. In addition to these short-term effects, such symptoms may also be early indicators of long-term consequences (if left untreated), such as osteoporosis and atherosclerosis.

In most cases, menopausal women do not have to suffer the effects of this hormonal

KNOWING WHEN TO PICK THE RIGHT HORSE: WHAT COULD BE MORE NATURAL? THE STORY OF PREMARIN®

deficiency. Women experiencing these unpleasant symptoms can greatly improve the quality of their lives by taking an estrogen product that will replace the estrogen their bodies lack. Wyeth-Ayerst has such a product—Premarin®. Premarin has been the standard in estrogen replacement therapy (ERT) for nearly 50 years.

A PHARMACEUTICAL MILESTONE

In January 1925, the pharmaceutical firm of Ayerst, McKenna & Harrison Co., Ltd., came to be in Newfoundland, Canada. The company's first product, introduced in 1929, was Alphamettes, the first cod liver oil concentrate in North America. By the early 1930s, the Ayerst product line had expanded to include not only cod liver oil, but also vitamin products, digitalis, phenobarbital, and a pituitary hormone product (A.P.L.®). Because so much business was crossing the border, Ayerst established an American branch of the company in 1934.

It was in the midst of this growth that a group of scientists at Ayerst and McGill University in Montreal collaborated and discovered the first orally active estrogen—Emmenin®. The company's source of estrogen used in the manufacturing of Emmenin was the urine from Canadian women who were in their last trimester of pregnancy. However, there were problems with this source (most notably, low activity, high cost, and odor and taste problems) which threatened the long-term survival of the product.

Dimensional
Illustrator: *Intervisual Communications*
Art Directors: *Scott Gross/Joel Sobelson*
Photographer: *Al Satterwhite*
Agency: *FCB/Leber Katz Partners*
Client: *R.J. Reynolds Tobacco/Salem Cigarettes*
Category: *Advertising Consumer Spread*

Dimensional
Illustrator: *Structural Graphics*
Art Directors: *Scott Gross/Joel Sobelson*
Photographer: *Greg Heisler*
Agency: *FCB/Leber Katz Partners*
Client: *R.J. Reynolds Tobacco/Salem Cigarettes*
Category: *Advertising Consumer Spread*

Dimensional
Illustrator: Angela Metzger
Art Director: Angela Metzger
Photographer: Rick Schindler/Belle Flair Schindler
Agency: N.M. Barnum & Associates, Ltd.
Client: Belleville Economic Progress Inc.
 Southwestern Illinois Tourism Bureau
Category: Advertising Direct Mail Brochure

Dimensional
Illustrator: Soren Thaae
Art Director: Jan Hovman
Photographer: Svend Lindbaek
Agency: Createam
Client: Baltica Insurance Company
Category: Newspaper

Dimensional
Illustrator: *Tim Nyberg*
Art Directors: *Tim Simmons/Eric Edward Brown*
Photographer: *Anthony Simmons*
Agency: *shoestring advertising/Tim Simmons Design*
Client: *Hennepin County Medical Society*
Category: *Magazine Advertising Full Page*

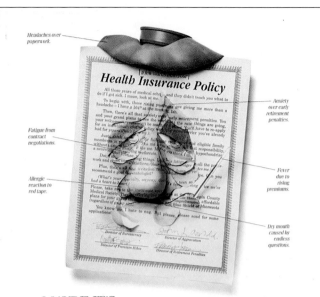

Dimensional
Illustrator: *Mark Crowe*
Art Director: *Mark Crowe*
Photographer: *K. Siemens*
Agency: *Siemens Photography*
Publisher: *Sierra On-Line Inc.*
Client: *Sierra On-Line Inc.*
Category: *Video Cover*

Dimensional
Illustrator: *Leo Monahan*
Art Director: *Ted Whitby*
Agency: *Kallir, Phillips, Ross, Inc.*
Client: *Ortho Pharmaceutical*
Category: *Advertising Business Brochure*

Dimensional
Illustrator: *Bob Shein*
Art Director: *Barbara Hennessy*
Publisher: *Viking Penguin, Inc.*
Client: *Viking Penguin, Inc.*
Category: *Advertising Direct Mail Poster*

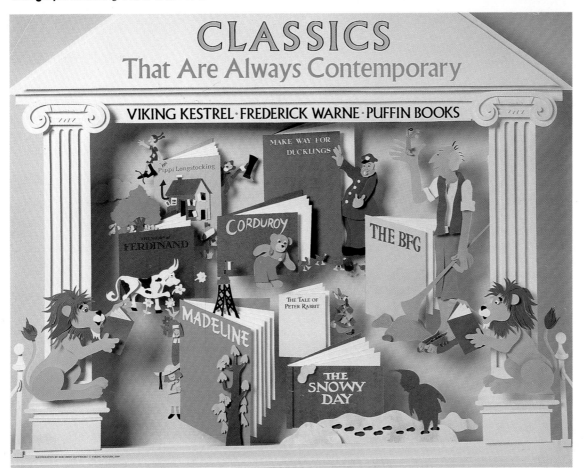

Dimensional
Illustrator: *Czeslaw Sornat*
Art Director: *Czeslaw Sornat*
Client: *Czeslaw Sornat*
Category: *Self Promotion*

czeslaw
sornat

Dimensional
Illustrator: *Toby Williams*
Art Director: *Toby Williams*
Photographer: *Bob Kramer*
Publisher: *WorkSource*
Category: *Self Promotion*

Dimensional
Illustrator: *Josje van Koppen*
Art Director: *Jan Brand*
Photographers: *Freek van Arkel & Pieter Vandermeer*
Agency: *Josje van Koppen Ontwerp & Illustratie*
Client: *ZilverenKruis Insurance*
Category: *Advertising Direct Mail Brochure*

Dimensional
Illustrator: *Andrew Nitzberg*
Art Director: *Curtis L Thomas*
Agency: *FCB/Leber Katz Partners*
Publisher: *Lenox*
Category: *Self Promotion*

45

Dimensional
Illustrators: *Bass & Goldman*
Art Directors: *Bass & Goldman*
Photographer: *Marvin Goldman*
Agency: *Bass & Goldman*
Category: *Self Promotion*

Dimensional
Illustrator: *Olive Alpert*
Art Directors: *Dale Fiorillo/Gerry Counihan*
Photographer: *Jelly Bean*
Publisher: *Dell Publishing*
Client: *Dell Publishing*
Category: *Illustration Editorial*

Dimensional
Illustrator: *Edward S.F. Chan*
Art Director: *Edward S.F. Chan*
Photographer: *Creative Men*
Agency: *Prime Productions House*
Category: *Self Promotion*

Dimensional
Illustrator: *Lisa Tysko*
Art Director: *Lisa Tysko*
Photographer: *Gamma One Conversions*
Category: *Self Promotion*

Dimensional
Illustrator: *Gus Alavezos*
Photographer: *Kevin Saehlenou*
Category: *Unpublished*

PAPER SCULPTURE

LISA TYSKO

7106 LAUREL COURT, MONMOUTH JUNCTION, NJ 08852 (201) 821-3057

Dimensional
Illustrator: *Joan Kritchman Knuteson*
Art Director: *Charles Ruggles*
Photographer: *Dick Baker*
Agency: *Advertising Art Studio*
Client: *International Institute*
Category: *Advertising Illustration Poster*

Dimensional
Illustrator: *Jerry Pavey*
Art Director: *Jerry Pavey*
Photographer: *William McCaw*
Agency: *Jerry Pavey Design & Illustration*
Publisher: *S & S Graphics, Inc.*
Client: *S.D. Warren Paper Co./S & S Graphics,Inc.*
Category: *Editorial Illustration*

Dimensional
Illustrator: *Janet Potter D'Amato*
Art Directors: *Sherry Fredy/Bob Chiriani*
Photographer: *Mark Metro*
Client: *Metro Creative Graphics*
Category: *Advertising Illustration*

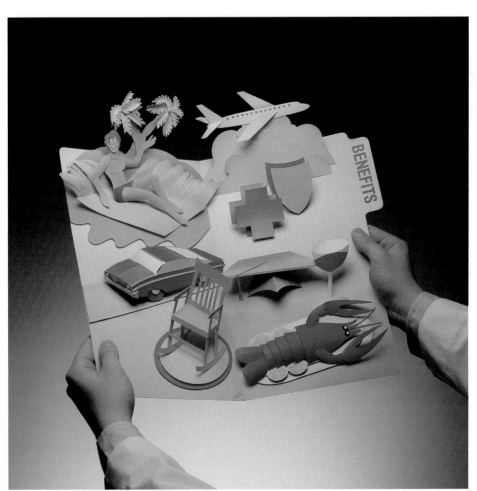

Dimensional
Illustrator: *Leo Monahan*
Art Director: *Roger Dowd*
Photographer: *Stephen Munz*
Agency: *Medical Economics Company*
Publisher: *Jim Jenkins*
Client: *Medical Economics Magazine*
Category: *Editorial Illustration*

Dimensional
Illustrator: *Gus Alavezos*
Art Director: *Marc Conly*
Photographer: *Kevin Saehlenou*
Agency: *Hart Publications*
Client: *Oil & Gas Investors*
Category: *Editorial Illustration*

Dimensional
Illustrator: *Hal Lose*
Art Director: *Hal Lose*
Photographer: *Howard Gale*
Agency: *Toad Hall Graphics*
Publisher: *American Showcase*
Client: *Hal Lose*
Category: *Illustration Advertising*

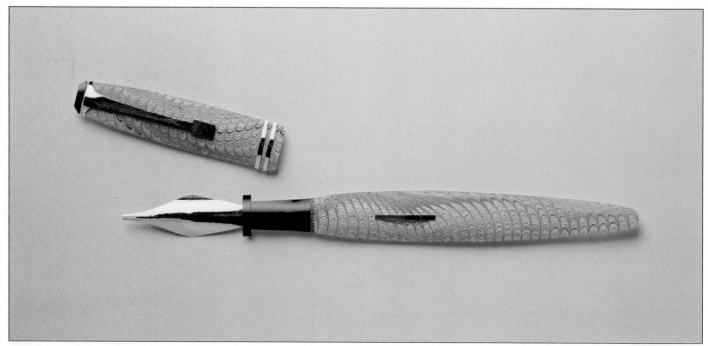

Dimensional
Illustrator: *Gus Alavezos*
Art Director: *Mark Wagner*
Photographer: *Kevin Saehlenou*
Agency: *Chiat/Day/Hoffer*
Client: *Intel*
Category: *Advertising Illustration*

Dimensional
Illustrator: *Mary Trachsel Hanson*
Art Director: *Mary Trachsel Hanson*
Photographer: *Julie Miller Walling*
Category: *Unpublished*

Dimensional
Illustrator: *Ajin*
Art Director: *Danielle Gallo*
Publisher: *Penthouse Letters*
Category: *Editorial Illustration*

Dimensional
Illustrator: *Ajin*
Art Director: *Danielle Gallo*
Publisher: *Penthouse Letters*
Category: *Editorial Illustration*

Dimensional
Illustrator: *Ajin*
Art Director: *Danielle Gallo*
Publisher: *Penthouse Letters*
Category: *Editorial Illustration*

Dimensional
Illustrator: *Ajin*
Art Director: *Danielle Gallo*
Publisher: *Penthouse Letters*
Category: *Editorial Illustration*

Dimensional
Illustrator: *Ajin*
Art Director: *Daniello Gallo*
Publisher: *Penthouse Letters*
Category: *Editorial Illustration*

Dimensional
Illustrator: *Ajin*
Art Director: *Danielle Gallo*
Publisher: *Penthouse Letters*
Category: *Editorial Illustration*

Dimensional
Illustrator: *Ajin*
Art Director: *Danielle Gallo*
Publisher: *Penthouse Letters*
Category: *Editorial Illustration*

Dimensional
Illustrator: *Ajin*
Art Director: *Danielle Gallo*
Publisher: *Penthouse Letters*
Category: *Editorial Illustration*

Dimensional
Illustrator: *Ajin*
Art Director: *Danielle Gallo*
Publisher: *Penthouse Letters*
Category: *Editorial Illustration*

Dimensional
Illustrator: *Tim Nyberg*
Art Director: *Sherry Reutiman*
Photographer: *Erik Saulitis*
Publisher: *Financial Publishers*
Client: *TCF Magazine*
Category: *Illustration Editorial*

Dimensional
Illustrator: *Ajin*
Art Director: *Danielle Gallo*
Publisher: *Penthouse Letters*
Category: *Editorial Illustration*

Dimensional
Illustrator: *Gus Alavezos*
Photographer: *Kevin Saehlenou*
Category: *Unpublished*

Dimensional
Illustrator: *Tim Nyberg*
Art Director: *Tim Nyberg*
Photographer: *Erik Saulitis*
Agency: *Many Hats, Inc.*
Category: *Illustration Editorial*

Dimensional
Illustrator: *Bill Finewood*
Art Director: *Marie Greco*
Photographer: *Bill Finewood*
Agency: *Art Works, Inc.*
Publisher: *Field Publications*
Category: *Editorial Illustration*

Dimensional
Illustrator: *Bill Finewood*
Art Director: *Jamie Bolane*
Photographer: *Jamey Stillings*
Agency: *Art Works, Inc.*
Publisher: *A Baby's Secret Garden*
Client: *Jamie Bolane*
Category: *Advertising Illustration Poster*

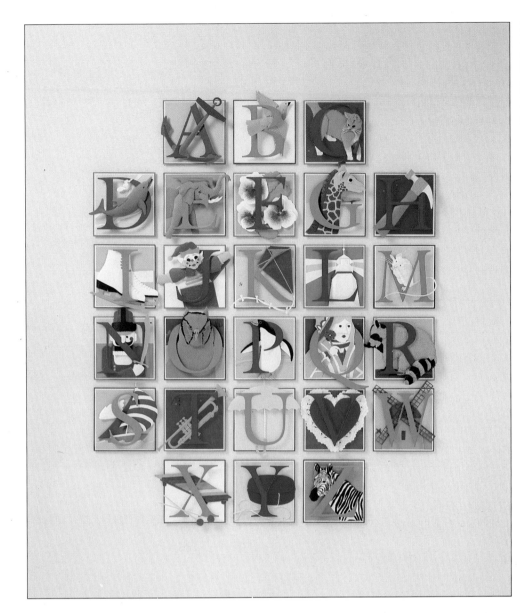

Dimensional
Illustrator: *Gus Alavezos*
Photographer: *Kevin Saehlenou*
Category: *Unpublished*

59

Dimensional
Illustrator: *Hal Lose*
Art Director: *Hal Lose*
Photographer: *Howard Gale*
Agency: *Toad Hall Graphics*
Publisher: *American Showcase*
Client: *Hal Lose*
Category: *Illustration Advertising*

Dimensional
Illustrator: *Bill Miller*
Art Director: *Bill Miller*
Photographer: *Bill Miller*
Agency: *Bill Miller*
Client: *Paper Classics*
Category: *Unpublished*

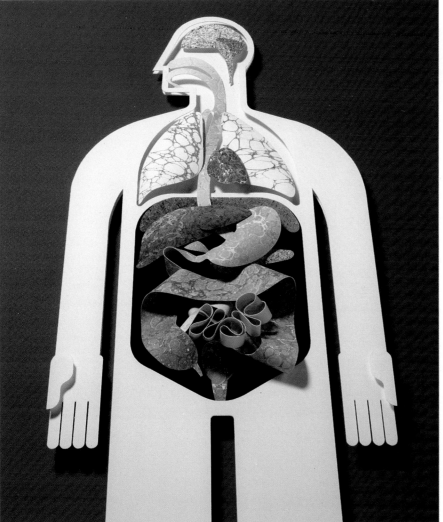

Dimensional
Illustrator: *Hal Lose*
Art Director: *Hal Lose*
Photographer: *Howard Gale*
Agency: *Toad Hall Graphics*
Publisher: *Adweek Portfolios*
Client: *Hal Lose*
Category: *Illustration Advertising*

Dimensional
Illustrator: *Bob Cowan*
Art Director: *Bob Cowan*
Photographer: *Bob Cowan*
Agency: *Bob Cowan*
Category: *Unpublished*

Dimensional
Illustrator: *Jef Workman*
Art Director: *Jef Workman*
Photographer: *Lee Hocker*
Agency: *Bird In The Hand Studio*
Client: *Bird In The Hand Studio*
Category: *Unpublished*

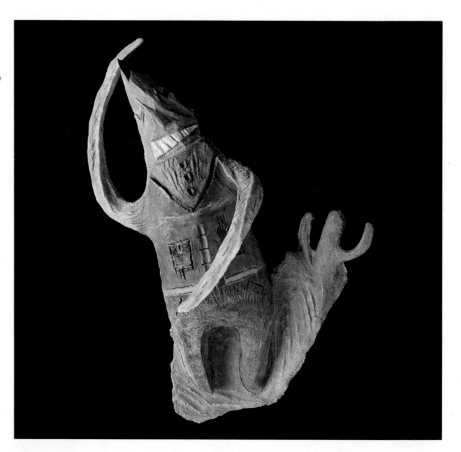

Dimensional
Illustrator: *Bob Cowan*
Art Director: *Bob Cowan*
Photographer: *Bob Cowan*
Agency: *Bob Cowan*
Category: *Unpublished*

Dimensional
Illustrator: *Joseph DeCerchio*
Art Director: *Joseph DeCerchio*
Photographer: *Bill Kovnat*
Agency: *JDC Designs*
Category: *Unpublished*

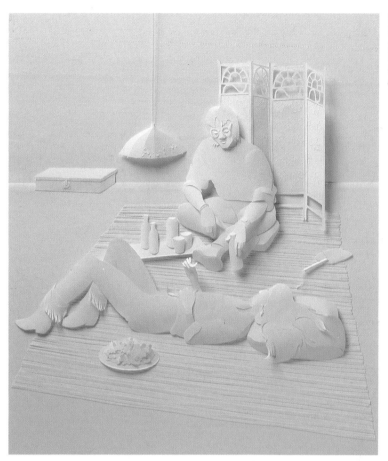

Dimensional
Illustrator: *Olive Alpert*
Art Director: *Olive Alpert*
Photographer: *Jelly Bean*
Client: *Olive Alpert*
Category: *Unpublished*

Dimensional
Illustrator: *Hal Lose*
Art Director: *Hal Lose*
Photographer: *Howard Gale*
Agency: *Toad Hall Graphics*
Publisher: *American Showcase*
Client: *Hal Lose*
Category: *Illustration Advertising*

Dimensional
Illustrator: *Johnna Bandle*
Art Director: *Dick Russinko*
Photographer: *John Olivo*
Agency: *Sudler & Hennessey*
Client: *Warner Lambert International*
Category: *Unpublished*

Dimensional
Illustrator: *Johnna Bandle*
Art Director: *Dick Russinko*
Photographer: *John Olivo*
Agency: *Sudler & Hennessey*
Client: *Warner Lambert International*
Category: *Unpublished*

Dimensional
Illustrator: *Bob Cowan*
Art Director: *Bob Cowan*
Photographer: *Bob Cowan*
Agency: *Bob Cowan*
Category: *Unpublished*

Dimensional
Illustrator: *Gus Alavezos*
Photographer: *Kevin Saehlenou*
Category: *Unpublished*

Dimensional
Illustrator: *Olive Alpert*
Art Director: *Olive Alpert*
Photographer: *Olive Alpert*
Agency: *Olive Alpert Design*
Category: *Unpublished*

Dimensional
Illustrator: *Tomm Scalera*
Art Director: *Tomm Scalera*
Photographer: *Tomm Scalera*
Category: *Greeting Card*

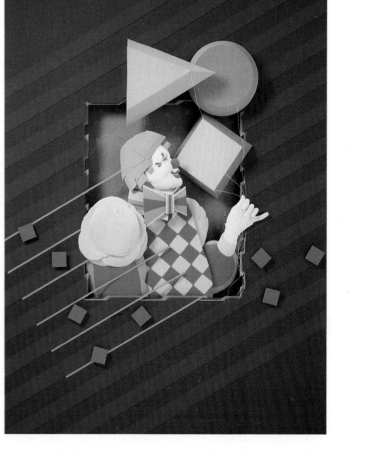

Dimensional
Illustrator: *Bill Finewood*
Art Director: *Bill Finewood*
Photographer: *Bill Finewood*
Agency: *Art Works, Inc.*
Publisher: *Strong Memorial Hospital*
Client: *Strong Children's Fund*
Category: *Greeting Card*

Dimensional
Illustrator: *Paul Schmitz*
Publisher: *Hallmark Cards, Inc.*
Category: *Greeting Card*

Dimensional
Illustrator: *R.E. Jordan*
Publisher: *Hallmark Cards, Inc.*
Category: *Greeting Card*

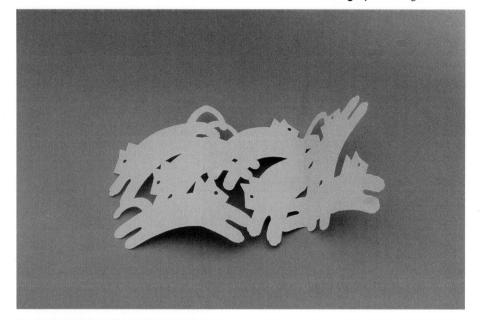

Dimensional
Illustrator: *R.E.Jordan*
Publisher: *Hallmark Cards, Inc.*
Category: *Greeting Card*

PAPER COLLAGE

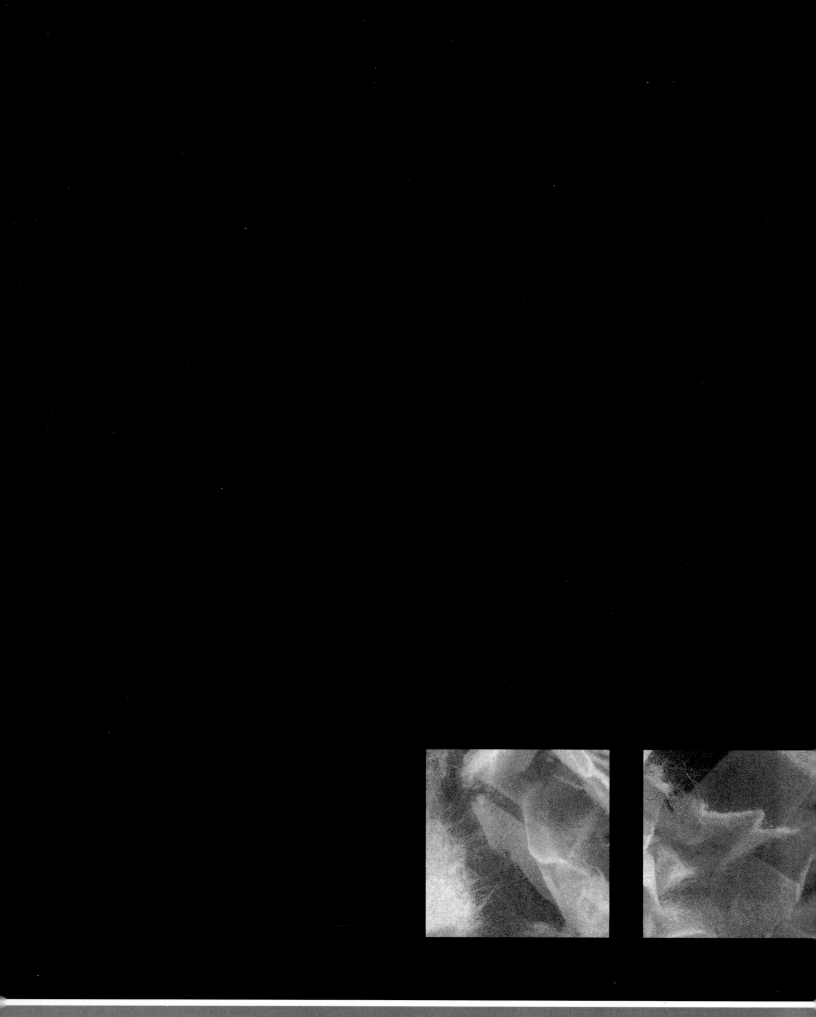

PAPER COLLAGE

IN TERMS OF ACTUAL DIMENSION, PAPER COLLAGE IS CONSIDERED A MINIMAL FORM OF 3-DIMENSIONAL ILLUSTRATION. THE ILLUSION OF DEPTH IS CREATED BY THE TECHNIQUES OF CUTTING OR TEARING PIECES OF PAPER, IMAGES OR PHOTOGRAPHS. DIMENSIONAL ARTISTS HAVE THE ABILITY TO INTEGRATE COLORS, TONES, TEXTURES AND PRINTED IMAGES WITH THE EXPLICIT FLATNESS OF PAPER TO CREATE STUNNING THREE-DIMENSIONAL ILLUSTRATIONS. THIS JUXTAPOSITION OF IMAGES COMMUNICATES THE ESSENCE OF PAPER COLLAGE.

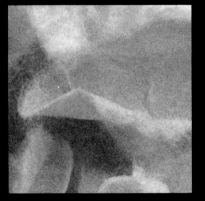

"You can make a point in a dimensional medium without getting lost in technicalities. A medical illustration of a heart will be looked at for quality and accuracy. A heart fashioned from wire and computer parts or one made of lucite will not be critiqued in the same way. Photographs and illustrations for print media are ends in themselves, ready for reproduction. It is ironic that the dimensional artist's work has to be de-dimensionalized (photographed) before its ready for print. However this step is another facet of the flexibility of this art form. It's about time that recognition be paid to this unique and evolving art form."

PAT CREAVEN

Dimensional
Illustrator: *Milton Glaser*
Art Director: *Milton Glaser*
Client: *School of Visual Arts*
Category: *Advertising Direct Mail Poster*

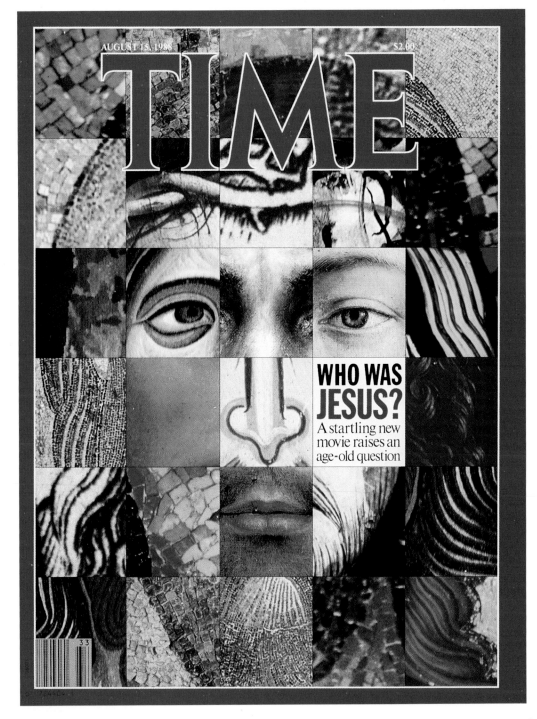

Dimensional
Illustrator: *Tom Bentkowski*
Art Director: *Rudolph Hoglund*
Publisher: *Time Incorporated*
Category: *Magazine Editorial Consumer Cover*

Dimensional
Illustrator: *Milton Glaser*
Art Director: *Milton Glaser*
Client: *The Art Directors Club*
Category: *Advertising Direct Mail Poster*

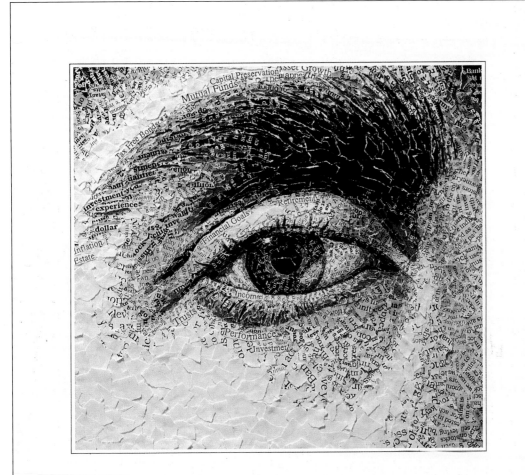

IN MANAGING YOUR ASSETS, WE GET YOUR POINT OF VIEW BEFORE WE GIVE YOU OURS.

Reaching a thorough understanding of your financial goals and investment objectives. That's where it all begins for our Personal Financial Managers in the SunBank Trust Banking Group.

That means listening very carefully to you. And only after we have an in-depth understanding do we get down to the business of translating your needs and goals into a personalized financial and investment program that performs.

This program can include everything from capital preservation to investments designed for growth. All the financial tools. And because we do not work on commission, we can be totally objective in giving advice and making investment recommendations.

In fact, our expertise and objectivity have made SunBank a consistent national leader in investment performance for the past ten years. That's why, from your point of view, it makes a lot of sense to contact SunBank soon and let us show you how we perform.

Sun Bank
Trust Banking

A SunTrust Bank ©1988 SunBanks, Inc.

Dimensional
Illustrator: Lauren Uram
Art Director: Gene Powers
Agency: Tucker Wayne
Client: Sun Bank
Category: Magazine Advertising Full Page

SILVER
AWARD

Dimensional
Illustrator: *Joan Hall*
Art Director: *Kathleen Forthyse*
Client: *Loomis, Sayles & Company*
Category: *Annual Report*

Dimensional
Illustrator: *Jacques Tosetto*
Art Director: *Jacques Tosetto*
Photographer: *Antoine Senne*
Category: *Illustration Advertising*

Dimensional
Illustrator: *Robert Rauschenberg*
Art Director: *Rudolph Hoglund*
Publisher: *Time Incorporated*
Category: *Editorial Magazine Consumer Cover*

Dimensional
Ilustrator: *Audrey Bernstein*
Art Director: *Rudolph Hoglund*
International Art Director: *Ina Saltz*
Publisher: *Time Incorporated*
Category: *Magazine Editorial Consumer Cover*

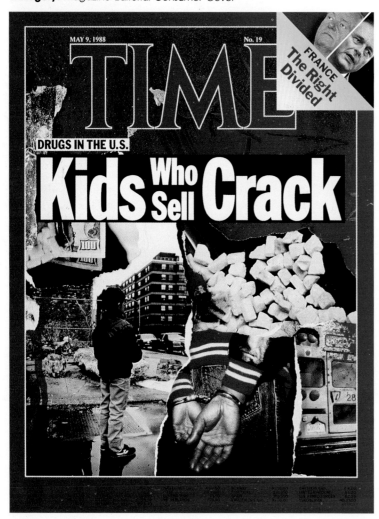

Dimensional
Illustrator: *Renee Klein*
Art Director: *Rudolph Hoglund*
Publisher: *Time Incorporated*
Category: *Magazine Editorial Consumer Cover*

Dimensional
Illustrator: *Marc Yankus*
Art Director: *Bessen & Tully*
Client: *Presbyterian Hospital*
Category: *Editorial Illustration*

Dimensional
Illustrator: *Lauren Uram*
Art Director: *Andrea DiBenedetto*
Agency: *Medical Economics Company*
Publisher: *Lee Hufnagel*
Client: *RN Magazine*
Category: *Editorial Magazine Business Cover*

Dimensional
Illustrator: *Lauren Uram*
Art Director: *Amy Bogart*
Publisher: *Matilda Publications Inc.*
Client: *Ms Magazine*
Category: *Magazine Editorial Business Full Page*

Dimensional
Illustrator: *Marc Yankus*
Art Director: *Ken Surabin*
Client: *Sales & Marketing Magazine*
Category: *Editorial Illustration*

Dimensional
Illustrator: *Milton Glaser*
Art Director: *Milton Glaser*
Client: *School of Visual Arts*
The First 40 Years
Category: *Advertising Direct Mail Poster*

Dimensional
Illustrator: *Cecily Lang*
Art Director: *Hans Van Reemst*
Publisher: *VNU Business Publicaitons*
Client: *Personal Computer Magazine*
Category: *Editorial Magazine Business Full Page*

Dimensional
Illustrator: *Cecily Lang*
Art Director: *Hans Van Reemst*
Publisher: *VNU Business Publications*
Client: *Personal Computer Magazine*
Category: *Editorial Illustration*

Dimensional
Illustrator: *Carol H. Norby*
Art Directors: *Mike Christian/Sonja Cowgill*
Publisher: *Novelle*
Client: *Lan Times*
Category: *Magazine Editorial Campaign*

Dimensional
Illustrator: Susan Baum
Art Director: Harriet Ziefert
Publisher: Puffin Books/Penguin Group
Category: Book

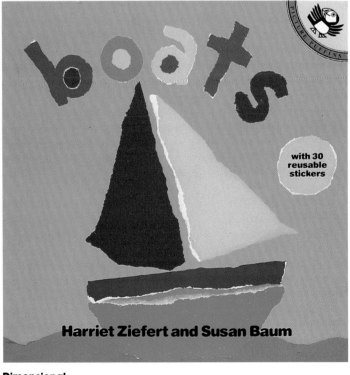

Dimensional
Illustrator: Susan Baum
Art Director: Harriet Ziefert
Publisher: Puffin Books/Penguin Group
Category: Book

Dimensional
Illustrator: *Carol H. Norby*
Art Director: *Ron Stucki*
Client: *Art Directors of Salt Lake City*
Category: *Advertising Direct Mail Consumer*

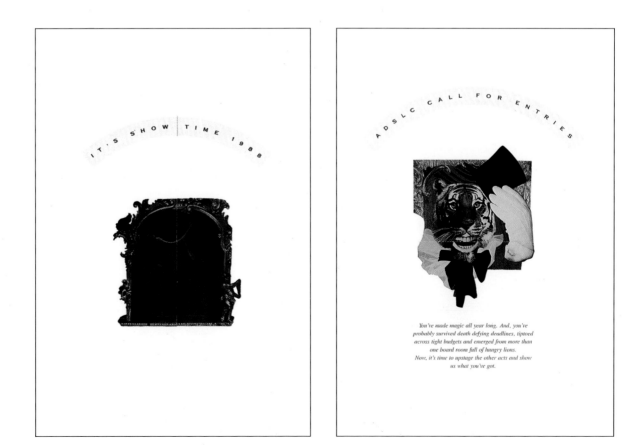

IT'S SHOW TIME 1988

ADSLC CALL FOR ENTRIES

You've made magic all year long. And, you've probably survived death defying deadlines, tiptoed across tight budgets and emerged from more than one board room full of hungry lions. Now, it's time to upstage the other acts and show us what you've got.

Dimensional
Illustrator: *Peter Nagy*
Art Director: *Donna Kwasnicki*
Photographer: *See Spot Run*
Agency: *Continental Golin/Harris Comm. Inc.*
Client: *Reed Stenhouse Ltd.*
Category: *Advertising Direct Mail Brochure*

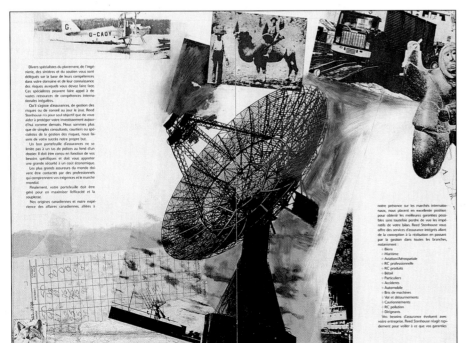

Dimensional
Illustrator: *Marc Yankus*
Art Director: *Clarke Thompson*
Client: *Business Week Careers*
Category: *Editorial Illustration*

Dimensional
Illustrator: *Marc Yankus*
Art Director: *Gene Moore*
Client: *Tiffany & Company*
Category: *Editorial Illustration*

Dimensional
Illustrator: *Lauren Uram*
Art Director: *Janice Brill*
Agency: *Cosmair*
Client: *Ralph Lauren*
Category: *Editorial Illustration*

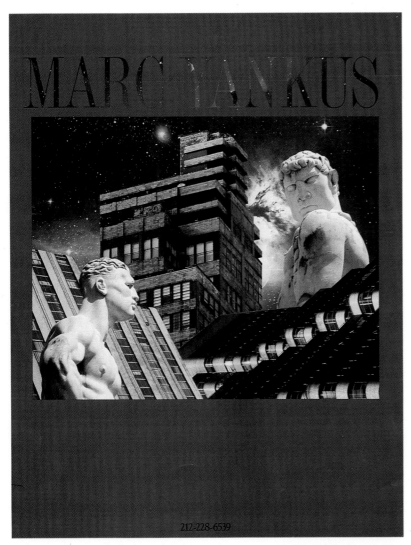

Dimensional
Illustrator: *Marc Yankus*
Designer: *Marc Yankus*
Client: *Marc Yankus*
Category: *Self Promotion*

Dimensional
Illustrator: *Cecily Lang*
Category: *Unpublished*

PLASTIC
SCULPTURE

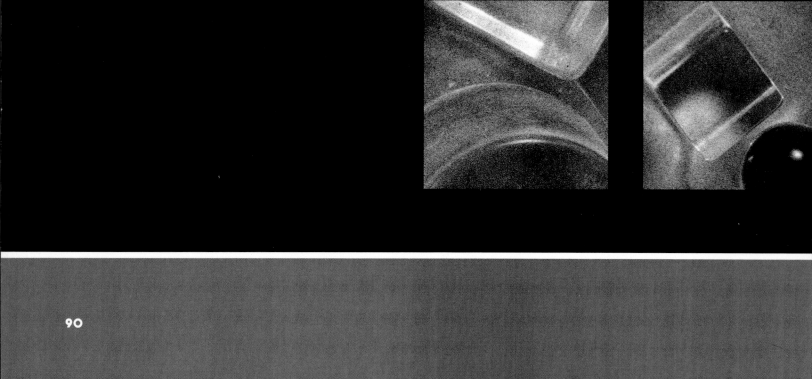

PLASTIC SCULPTURE

MODELS FABRICATED FROM PLASTIC PROVIDE A VARIETY OF STRUCTURAL SOLUTIONS FOR THE 3-DIMENSIONAL ILLUSTRATOR. THE MACHINING TECHNIQUES UTILIZED IN THIS RIGID MEDIUM REQUIRE THE SKILLS, PRECISION AND EXPERTISE OF HIGHLY SOPHISTICATED MODELMAKERS. THESE UNIQUE ARTISANS CONSTRUCT MODELS, PROPS, SETS, AND PLASTIC ASSEMBLAGES THUS PRO- VIDING SOLUTIONS THAT ARE IMPOSSIBLE TO REPRODUCE 2-DIMENSIONALLY. NEW TECHNO- LOGICAL ADVANCES IN PLASTIC MATERIALS ARE PROVIDING MODELMAKERS NEW AND UNLIMITED ILLUSTRATIVE POSSIBILITIES. THE HIGH-TECH QUALITY OF PLASTIC ENHANCES THE APPEAL OF THE ILLUSTRATION, PRESENTS A STRIKING AES- THETIC IMAGERY AND SATISFIES THE DEMANDS OF TODAY'S COSMOPOLITAN CONSUMERS.

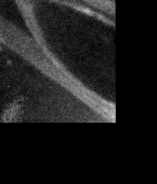

"I am very much aware that three-dimensional illustration is becoming more of a presence today. Seeing more and more pop-up ads in magazines, it would appear we have embarked on a "can you top this" trend in print advertising, driven by highly imaginative uses of three-dimensional illustration. The California Raisins, notwithstanding, Claymation® has been with us for years, but the current popularity of that art form is staggering. So, I expect we will see much more utilization of dimensional design and illustration in the future in advertising."
LOU DIJOSEPH

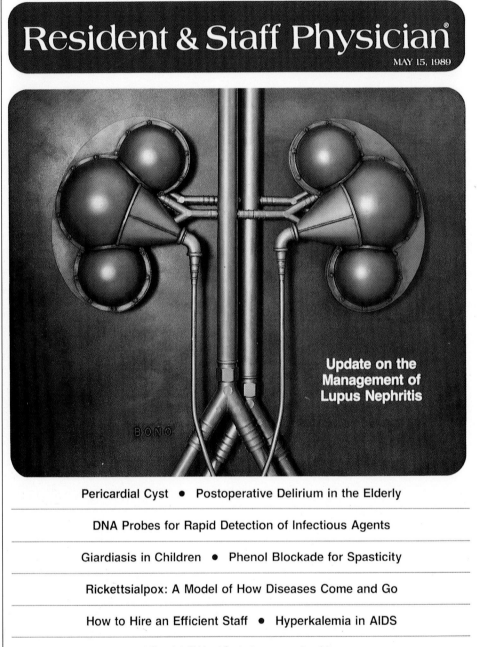

Dimensional
Illustrator: *Mary M. Bono*
Art Director: *Frank Schmitz*
Photographer: *Mary M. Bono*
Executive Editor: *Anne Mattarella*
Publisher: *Romaine Pierson Publishers, Inc.*
Client: *Resident & Staff Physician*
Category: *Editorial Magazine Business Cover*

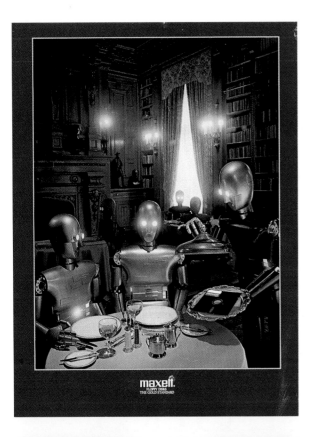

Dimensional
Illustrator: *Michael Maniatis*
Art Director: *George Pouridis*
Photographer: *David Langley*
Agency: *AC&R*
Category: *Advertising Direct Mail Campaign*

THE FUTURE IS PLASTICS, BUT WHERE WILL IT END?

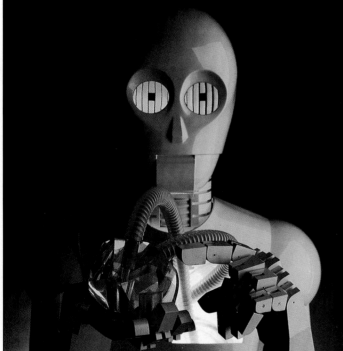

You're part of one of the fastest growing industries in the world. Every day plastics are becoming more and more an essential part of life. And who knows, soon there may even be walking, talking plastic robots.

Sound scary? It could be. If you're not ready to take advantage of the opportunities plastics have to offer.

Introducing The Conair Group.

We're a select group of companies devoted specifically to meeting the needs of the plastics processing industry. Both now and in the future. The Conair Group designs, builds and installs a full line of equipment and systems for water management, scrap granulation and robotic parts handling. We offer downstream extrusion auxiliaries, resin conveying and storage, polymer filtration, pelletizers and scrap reclamation systems. And we can do it all for you, anywhere in the world.

The Conair Group also helps you plan for the equipment needs of your extrusion, injection molding, compounding or blow molding operation. We offer turnkey auxiliary equipment systems, leasing, training, field service and spares. And we deliver. On time. Guaranteed.

In plastics, the sky's the limit. Get in on the ground floor with The Conair Group. For more information, call (800) 289-1289. Or write The Conair Group, 20 Stanwix Street, Pittsburgh, PA 15222.

Conair Franklin
Conair Jetro
Conair Churchill
Conair Pacific
Conair Martin
Conair Kawata
Conair Extrusion
Conair Leasing
Conair Gatto
Conair Martin, U.K.

We Guarantee Performance.

THE CONAIR GROUP

Dimensional
Illustrator: *The Objects Works*
Art Director: *George Titonis*
Photographer: *Tim Prendergast*
Agency: *Ketchum Advertising*
Client: *The Conair Group*
Category: *Magazine Advertising Business Spread*

Dimensional
Illustrator: *The Object Works*
Art Director: *Len Tucci*
Photographer: *Walt Seng*
Agency: *Della Femina McNamee WCRS, Inc.*
Client: *Federated Investors Inc.*
Category: *Advertising Direct Mail Brochure*

Dimensional
Illustrator: *Kathleen Ziegler*
Art Director: *Jake Smith*
Photographer: *Bob Emmott*
Publisher: *Springhouse Corporation*
Client: *Learning '88*
Category: *Magazine Editorial Business Cover*

Dimensional
Illustrator: *Kathleen Ziegler*
Art Director: *Edward Rosanio*
Photographer: *Eric Pervukhin*
Publisher: *Springhouse Corporation*
Client: *Nursing '87*
Category: *Magazine Editorial Business Cover*

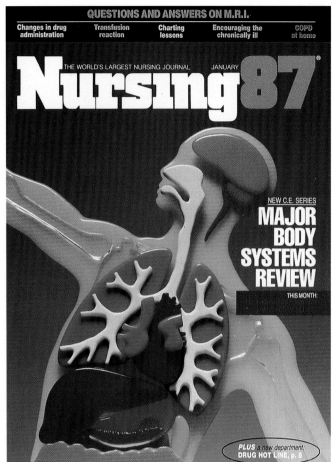

Dimensional
Illustrator: *Kathleen Ziegler*
Art Director: *Edward Rosanio*
Photographer: *Eric Pervukhin*
Publisher: *Springhouse Corporation*
Client: *Nursing '87*
Category: *Magazine Editorial Campaign*

ASSESSING THE
FAILING STATE OF THE HEART

Continuing our CE theme on body systems, we take a look this month at the mechanical side of the cardiovascular system—and what happens when nature's most astonishing pump starts to fail.

ANA/AACN-APPROVED

BY EILEEN VAN PARYS, RN, MSN
Curriculum Coordinator
School of Nursing
Abington Hospital
Abington, Pennsylvania

42 Nursing87, February

ANYONE who's ever stared helplessly at a stalled car engine knows: You can't fix something that's broken unless you understand how it works in the first place.

This is especially true with something as complex and vital as the human heart. To assess the patient with a failing heart that can't pump enough blood to meet metabolic demands, you first need to understand how the heart normally works. Not only will this help you anticipate signs and symptoms, it'll also give you a sound physiologic basis for interpreting the significance of your assessment findings.

Compensatory mechanisms
The key to understanding heart failure is to think of the heart as a two-sided pump. The quantity of blood the left ventricle pumps each minute into the aorta (or the right ventricle pumps into the pulmonary artery) depends on the ventricle's rate of contraction and the volume of blood it pumps with each contraction or stroke. This relationship is expressed in the formula: Cardiac output = heart rate x stroke volume.

When either heart rate or stroke volume varies, the other compensates to keep cardiac output stable. For instance, if heart rate slows, lengthening diastole (relaxation) and filling time, the heart can make up for it during systole (contraction) by ejecting more blood with each beat. Similarly, if stroke volume drops, a faster heart rate will keep cardiac output fairly constant. These compensatory mechanisms are described more fully in the insert *Controlling Heart Rate and Stroke Volume.*

Various conditions—both acute and chronic—can push the heart's compensatory mechanisms beyond their limits. One such acute condition is myocardial infarction (MI). For at least the first 6 hours after an MI, the damaged part of the heart muscle, inelastic but not yet fibrous, puffs out paradoxically whenever the ventricle contracts. This markedly reduces the heart's contractility and thus its output.

Chronic heart failure develops when a damaged chamber gradually enlarges and loses contractility. Conditions leading to chronic heart failure include ischemic heart disease, arteriosclerosis, hypertension, cardiac valve disease, congenital heart disease, massive circulatory overload from kidney failure, and low PaO₂ levels from respiratory disease or anemia.

The hallmark of heart failure, whatever its cause, is a reduced ventricular ejection fraction. The ventricle normally ejects 60% to 70% of the blood it contained at end diastole. With heart failure, it ejects less than that, thus increasing the volume of blood remaining inside it. The resulting signs and symptoms depend on which ventricle is first involved and how severe the failure is.

Effects of left- and right-sided failure
As we discuss left- and right-sided failure, keep in mind that the heart, although divided into two, functions as a single organ. Changes in one side affect the other, partly because of continuous muscle fibers and electric pathways. Stress, coronary artery disease, or other factors influencing stroke volume and heart rate affect both ventricles, although not to the same degree.

Another point to remember is that pressure changes resulting from failure in the left or right side—or in both—are reflected forward and backward. Forward failure from the left ventricle reduces blood flow through the aorta to the systemic circulation, producing ischemia of the myocardium, kidneys, and brain. Left-sided backward failure increases pressure in the pulmonary vascular system. The result? Pulmonary congestion.

Most ventricular failures occur in the left side. Generally, however, primary left-sided ventricular failure eventually leads to secondary right-sided failure. That's because the right ventricle and atrium must struggle to pump against the pulmonary congestion caused by left-sided failure.

Primary right ventricular failure can result from right ventricular MI or pulmonary conditions such as chronic obstructive pulmonary disease or pulmonary artery stenosis. Right-sided failure also has its forward and backward effects. Forward failure from the right ventricle decreases blood flow through the pulmonary artery to the lungs. Backward failure leads to congestion in the superior and inferior venae cavae and eventually the venous system. Fluid shifts from the circulation to extravascular tissue spaces, causing ankle or sacral edema and fluid accumulation in body cavities (ascites, for example). In time, congestion of the liver and gastrointestinal (GI) tract may result.

The chart, *Heart Failure: What Happens and What to Look For,* will give you more information on these forward and backward effects of left- and right-sided heart failure.

Risk factors for heart failure
If your patient's condition permits, begin your assessment with a health history. Try to find out whether he's had an MI—heart failure is a serious complication of MI, with a death rate of 33%. Other conditions that put a patient at risk for heart failure are hypertension, coronary artery disease,

Nursing87 VOLUME 17, NUMBER 1, JANUARY 1987

DIABETES
NEW NAMES, NEW TEST, NEW DIET

This article introduces our continuing education theme for 1987—a comprehensive review of body systems. Each month, we'll examine a specific form of pathology that results from the breakdown of a different system. This month—diabetes mellitus and the endocrine system.

Earn CEUs
ANA/AACN-APPROVED

BY CLAUDIA CHRISTMAN, CPT, RN, BSN
Adult Nurse Practitioner
Silas B. Hayes Army Community Hospital
Fort Ord, California

JULIE BENNETT, RN, BSN
Community Health Nurse
Lutheran Medical Center
Home Health Services
Wheatridge, Colorado

DIABETES MELLITUS is a dynamic disease, notorious for its fluctuations in severity. Care of the diabetic patient mirrors the disease. It keeps changing, evolving, as research continues and new protocols are established.

Are you up-to-date on recent advances in understanding and controlling diabetes? This article will help you make sure you are. And, just as important, it'll help you get your diabetic patient involved in his care. You're well aware of the importance of patient teaching in managing diabetes. So keep in mind that the information we'll be covering here needs to be passed on to the patient.

IDDM: More severe form
As you probably know, what used to be known as juvenile-onset or ketosis-prone diabetes is now called *Type I, insulin-dependent diabetes mellitus* (IDDM). And what was previously termed adult-onset or ketosis-resistant diabetes is now called *Type II, non-insulin-dependent diabetes mellitus* (NIDDM).

The pathophysiology behind the two types of diabetes reflects a breakdown in the endocrine system, specifically pancreatic function. We won't go into that here, but the insert *How the Endocrine System Works* will spell it out for you in detail.

The important thing to remember is that with IDDM, the islets of Langerhans in the pancreas are smaller and fewer than normal, and they produce virtually no insulin at all. The patient needs exogenous insulin to survive. When you think of IDDM, think "young people." (Remember its old name—juvenile-onset diabetes.) Most patients with this type of diabetes are teenagers when the disease is first diagnosed.

Patients with IDDM account for only 10% to 15% of all diabetic patients. But they can get into trouble in a hurry; signs and symptoms of IDDM usually develop abruptly.

What to look for? The most common signs and symptoms of IDDM are polyuria, polydipsia, polyphagia (excessive hunger), weight loss, weakness, and fatigue. But the big danger with this type of diabetes is ketoacidosis. (Remember the other name IDDM used to go by—ketosis-prone diabetes.) Deprived of glucose because of the lack of insulin, the body must get its energy mostly from fats. The metabolism of these fats produces ketone bodies—very strong acids that accumulate in the blood, producing potentially life-threatening effects such as diabetic coma.

NIDDM: More common form
The odds are, however, that your diabetic patient will have NIDDM. Nearly 90% of all diabetic patients have this less severe form of the disease. Their underlying abnormality is not an absolute insufficiency of insulin, as with IDDM, but a relative insufficiency. The islets of Langerhans aren't reduced in size or number; in fact, the patient with NIDDM may have more islets than normal, apparently because of excessive demands for insulin over many years. And the islets do produce insulin.

The problem is that the amount of insulin produced by a person with NIDDM is less than a nondiabetic person produces. Or—another possibility—his pancreas may produce an adequate amount of insulin (or even an above-average amount), but the insulin doesn't have the effect it should because insulin receptor sites have become insensitive to it.

When you think of NIDDM, think "older people" and "obesity," because this type of diabetes is most often seen in older adults (over 40) who are overweight. They usually don't have any obvious signs and symptoms, unlike IDDM patients. Typically, their diabetes develops gradually and is eventually discovered by routine screening tests. They're far less likely to develop ketoacidosis. In severe cases, however, these patients may have polyuria, polydipsia, drowsiness, fatigue, blurred vision, weight loss, muscle cramps, and persistent infections.

Diagnosing and monitoring diabetes
The diagnosis of diabetes mellitus is based on blood glucose levels, using precise criteria established by the National Diabetes Data Group of the National Institutes of Health (see chart *Criteria for Diagnosing Diabetes Mellitus*). Frequent monitoring of glucose levels also figures prominently in managing the disease.

For both types of diabetes, the goal of treatment is to maintain fasting blood sugar (FBS) levels within a fairly narrow range—80 to 115 mg/dl. If your diabetic patient can keep his glucose level consistently within this range, he should be able to minimize long-term complications. But a lot of factors come into play—age, stress, infection, existing complications, and the patient's ability to care for himself.

The tests most often used to diagnose or monitor diabetes are the oral glucose tolerance test, the FBS test, the 2-hour postprandial test, the 4 p.m. blood glucose test, and the random blood glucose test.

Another way to monitor the diabetic patient is to use urine specimens for semiquantitative measurements of glucose levels. Urine tests, however, aren't as precise as blood tests, so you can't rely on

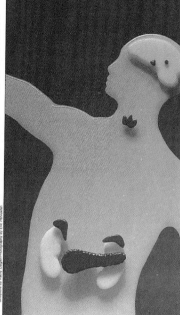
Sculpture by Kathy Ziegler/Photography by Eric Pendelton

A MODEL APPROACH TO
PAIN ASSESSMENT

Built around four key factors, the model proposed here will help you assess your patient's pain with greater precision.

Earn CEUs
ANA/AACN-APPROVED

BY GAYLE OLSSON, RN, MN
Staff-Development Specialist
Division of Nursing

GRACE PARKER, RNC, MN
Nurse Coordinator
Pain Clinic

University Hospital
University of Washington
Seattle, Washington

TWO DAYS after her right leg was amputated above the knee because of osteosarcoma, Colleen Wilson seems to be doing well. A moderate amount of serosanguineous fluid drains from the wound. She's afebrile and hasn't been complaining of pain.

For the first 12 hours after the operation, the 19-year-old college student had been using a patient-controlled analgesia (PCA) unit to administer about 5 mg of morphine intravenously (I.V.) every hour. Over the next 36 hours, her morphine use dropped to approximately 2.5 mg an hour.

No one suspects that anything is wrong. But Mark, Colleen's boyfriend, sees the mask drop when the nurses aren't around. He approaches Gloria, Colleen's primary nurse, in the hall and expresses his concerns.

"She's just not herself," Mark says. "She's crying a lot. And hurting real bad."

If you were Gloria, hurrying down the hall to check on Colleen, you'd have a lot of questions running through your mind. Does Colleen need more pain medication? Is there a problem with the stump? You might even wonder if this was Colleen's way of manipulating for more medication.

Assessment tool you can use
Pain assessment is the grayest of gray areas in nursing. Trying to help sick people feel more comfortable is no simple matter. How much pain medication is enough? What other measures can be used to alleviate a patient's pain? And when should you use them?

The answers to these questions won't come to you out of the blue. You have to work to uncover them, using a focused approach to pain assessment. That's what we'd like to present here—a specific "pain

model" that will help you assess your patient's pain systematically.

We've found the model developed by Loeser to be an excellent tool for organizing and analyzing pain assessment data. The Loeser model suggests that you consider four factors when assessing pain: *nociception*, *pain*, *suffering*, and *pain behaviors*. These factors can all contribute to the experience of pain. They build on one another and must all be considered when assessing pain (see diagram).

Let's take a look at each factor. Then we'll get back to Colleen and demonstrate how the model can be used.

Nociception:
Nervous system activation
You can think of *nociception*, the first factor to consider, as strictly a peripheral event. There's a sliver of wood under your thumbnail; the free nerve endings in your thumb detect its presence and send pain signals to the central nervous system. That's nociception.

When assessing for nociception, think in terms of tissue damage that has activated the nervous system. You want to ask yourself the questions: "What is happening in this patient's body tissues? What is initiating pain signals?"

Specifically, you're looking for actual or potential tissue damage from thermal, mechanical, or chemical causes. Some examples of such causes would be infection, inflammation, bowel or bladder distension, and physical trauma from a nasogastric tube or an I.V. catheter.

Pain: How do you know it's present?
As a result of nociception, noxious stimuli are transmitted to the central nervous system. And your patient feels *pain*.

But how do you *know* she's in pain? What tells you she's in pain? These are the key questions you want to ask yourself when considering this second assessment factor in the pain model.

There are two ways to know that a patient is in pain. The first is subjective: The patient tells you she's in pain. She describes what she's feeling and she calls it pain. The second is objective: For example, you find signs of sympathetic nervous system activation, such as changes in blood pressure, heart rate, or respiratory status.

Suffering: Emotional impact
Although *suffering* is not synonymous with pain, people often talk in terms of pain when they discuss suffering. They have trouble talking about suffering itself, perhaps because they don't have the vocabulary for it; they find it hard to put their emotions into words. It's easier for them to talk in terms of pain.

But people *show* suffering in many different ways. Anxiety, fear, anger, depression, stoic endurance—these are all ways in which people express suffering. Often their feelings are related to a sense of loss—the loss of a job, for example, or an alteration in body image.

So the key question you want to ask yourself when assessing for suffering is: "How is the pain affecting this patient emotionally?"

Pain behaviors:
Measurable and changeable
A patient's *pain behaviors* are her way of telling you she's in pain. They are very individualized, shaped by the patient's personality and background. Cultural and social factors come into play.

Pain behaviors are measurable—for ex-

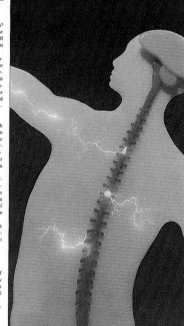
Sculpture by Kathy Ziegler/Photography by Eric Pendelton

Dimensional
Illustrator: *Nick Aristovulos*
Art Director: *Patrick Creaven*
Photographer: *Shig Ikeda*
Agency: *William Douglas McAdams*
Client: *Janssen Pharm*
Category: *Advertising Magazine Full Page*

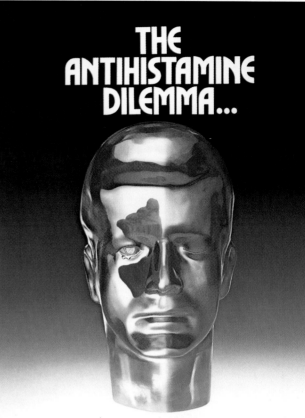

Soon to be resolved with
a new product from Janssen Pharmaceutica.

Dimensional
Illustrator: *Nick Aristovulos*
Art Director: *Patrick Creaven*
Photographer: *Shig Ikeda*
Agency: *William Douglas McAdams*
Client: *Janssen Pharmaceutica*
Category: *Advertising Magazine Business Spread*

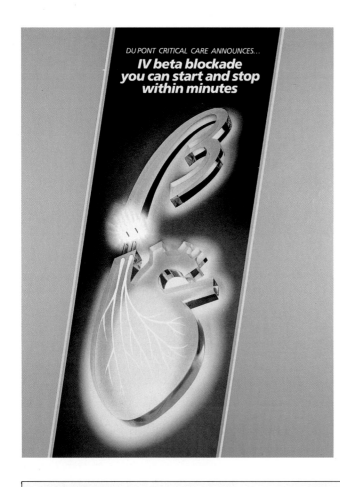

Dimensional
Illustrator: *Nick Aristovulos*
Art Director: *Patrick Creaven*
Photographer: *Shig Ikeda*
Agency: *William Douglas McAdams*
Client: *Dupont Critical Care*
Category: *Advertising Magazine Full Page*

Dimensional
Illustrators: *Mark Yurkiw Ltd. Staff*
Art Director: *Ralph Abreu*
Photographer: *Hashi*
Agency: *Arthur Kramer Advertising*
Client: *Marchon*
Category: *Magazine Advertising Full Page*

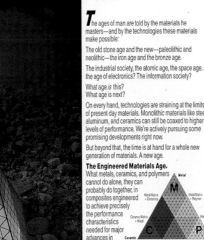

Dimensional
Illustrator: *The Object Works*
Art Director: *David Gates*
Photographer: *Photosynthesis*
Agency: *Vandine Horton McNamara Manges*
Client: *Alcoa*
Category: *Magazine Advertising Full Page*

Dimensional
Illustrator: *Nick Aristovulos*
Art Director: *Dick Russinko*
Photographer: *John Olivo*
Agency: *Sudler & Hennessey*
Publisher: *Lasky Printing*
Client: *Berlex Laboratories*
Category: *Advertising Direct Mail Brochure*

NEW *Magnevist*®
(gadopentetate dimeglumine) INJECTION

THE FIRST
PARAMAGNETIC
ENHANCEMENT
AGENT FOR *MRI*

BERLEX
IMAGING™

NEW *Magnevist*®
(gadopentetate dimeglumine) INJECTION

BETTER MEDICINE
THROUGH BETTER IMAGES

Delineates and defines lesions. In clinical trials, which included double-blind as well as open-label controlled studies, post-MAGNEVIST® injection T1 scans showed quantitative increase in contrast, differentiating surrounding tissue from mass lesion.[1]

Contrast enhancement to facilitate diagnosis
In the majority of patients, diagnostic ability was facilitated or improved by enhanced contrast with MAGNEVIST® injection.

CONTRAST ENHANCEMENT TO FACILITATE DIAGNOSIS[1]

Type of Study	No. of Patients	%
Double-blind	37/57	**65**
Open-label	70/113	**62**

Increased number of lesions detected
In 24% (92/388) of patients, post-MAGNEVIST® injection scans showed an increase in the number of lesions detected in double-blind and open-label clinical studies.

NUMBER OF LESIONS DETECTED[1]

Result of Study	Type of Study	MAGNEVIST® injection No. of Patients	%
Increased no. of lesions postinjection	Double-blind	10/43*	**23**
	Open-label	16/113*	**14**
Lesions seen postinjection but not preinjection	Open-label	66/232	**28**
	Total	92/388	**24**

*The question was answered only for patients with contrast enhancement.

1. Data on file, Berlex Laboratories, Inc.
   Please see full prescribing information for MAGNEVIST® injection on pages 10 and 11 of this folder.

BERLEX
IMAGING™

Dimensional
Illustrator: *Nick Aristovulos*
Art Director: *Dick Russinko*
Photographer: *John Olivo*
Agency: *Sudler & Hennessey*
Publisher: *Lasky Printing*
Client: *Berlex Laboratories*
Category: *Advertising Direct Mail Brochure*

Magnevist (gadopentetate dimeglumine) INJECTION

NOW INDICATED
FOR MRI OF THE SPINE

IMPROVES LESION DETECTION AND DEPICTION

Following MAGNEVIST® injection, T1-weighted MRI scans provide contrast enhancement to facilitate diagnosis of lesions in the spine and associated tissue characterized by abnormal vascularity or disruption of the blood-brain barrier.

USEFULNESS BEYOND DIAGNOSIS

MAGNEVIST® injection is useful in the diagnosis of intramedullary, intradural/extramedullary and extradural tumors. In 90% (52/58) of patients with postoperative back pain, the additional information was shown to affect recommended therapy.[1]

© 1989, Berlex Laboratories, Inc.   All rights reserved.

OVERALL RESULTS IN 169 PATIENTS FROM
MULTICENTER AND SINGLE-CENTER STUDIES

● Contrast enhancement was demonstrated for **85%** (144/169) of patients studied*[1]

● Additional radiologic information about the location, size or configuration of the lesions was provided in **78%** (131/169) of patients[1]

● In **29%** (21/73) of patients with suspected spinal lesions, the additional information consisted of a change in the number of lesions seen[1]

● In **95%** (55/58) of patients with recurrent postoperative back pain, MAGNEVIST® injection made it possible to better distinguish scar tissue from disc[1]

WELL TOLERATED

Most of the adverse reactions reported were mild and of short duration. Of 190 patients, the most common adverse reaction reported was injection-site coldness in 26 patients (13.7%). The second most common adverse reaction was headache, which was reported in 12 patients (6.3%). In these clinical trials, 6% to 8% of patients experienced an asymptomatic transient rise in serum iron.[1]

*Of the 169 patients who were evaluated, 111 had suspected spinal lesions and 58 presented with recurrent postoperative back pain.

1. Data on file, Berlex Laboratories, Inc.

Please see full prescribing information for MAGNEVIST® injection on last inside pages of this folder.

Dimensional
Illustrators: *Mark Yurkiw Ltd. Staff*
Photographer: *Steve Bronstein*
Agency: *FCB/Leber Katz Partners*
Client: *Salem*
Category: *Magazine Advertising Full Page*

Dimensional
Illustrator: *The Object Works*
Art Director: *Don Kress*
Photographer: *Walt Seng*
Agency: *Della Femina McNamee WCRS, Inc.*
Client: *Bayer USA, Inc.*
Category: *Magazine Advertising Business Spread*

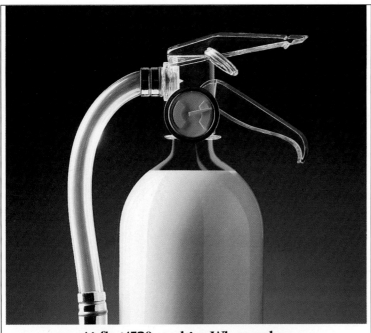

Airflex 4530 emulsion. What you buy if you want flame retardance in nonwovens.

Airflex 4530 ethylene-vinyl chloride emulsion may just be the best flame retardant binder you can buy. You see, its unique chemistry makes it inherently flame resistant. And, when combined with typically used flame retardant additives, it also provides better flame resistance than almost any combination of binder and flame retardant additive that we tested.

We have the data to prove it.

The tests took a hard look at every major class of binder used in nonwovens. Acrylic. SBR. PVC. Vinyl acrylic. Polyvinyl acetate. And every

major flame retardant additive. You'd recognize the names.

For both vertical and horizontal burn, Airflex 4530 emulsion/flame retardant additive combinations provided significantly more protection in both durable and nondurable formulations. Overall, no other binder was even in our league.

And you don't have to give up other properties to get a binder this good.

Along with great flame retardance, we can promise high wet and dry strength, abrasion resistance, and heat sealing capability. Airflex 4530

emulsion can even be crosslinked with other resins.

Clear superiority is often hard to come by. Airflex 4530 emulsion has it. We want to prove it to you by sending you a copy of the tests and a sample. To get yours, write Air Products and Chemicals, Inc., P.O. Box 538, Allentown, Pennsylvania 18105. Or call (215) 481-7027.
© Air Products and Chemicals, Inc., 1986

More than chemicals. Chemistry.

AIR PRODUCTS

Dimensional
Illustrator: *Bob Emmott*
Art Director: *Laurie Miller*
Photographer: *Bob Emmott*
Agency: *Lewis Gilman & Kynett*
Client: *Air Products & Chemicals*
Category: *Magazine Advertising Full Page*

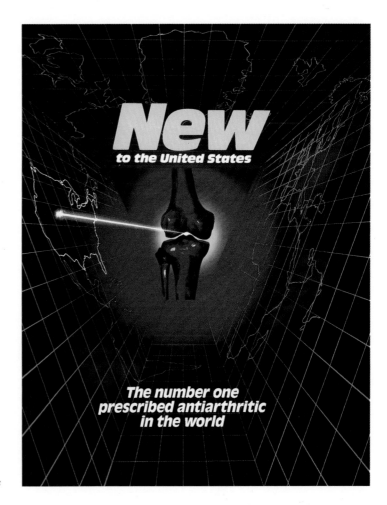

Dimensional
Illustrators: *Mark Yurkiw Ltd. Staff*
Art Director: *Mike Lazur*
Photographer: *Carmine Macedonia*
Agency: *Salthouse Torre Norton Inc.*
Client: *Ciba-Geigy*
Category: *Advertising Direct Mail Business*

Dimensional
Illustrator: *The Object Works*
Art Director: *Craig Otto*
Photographer: *Tim Prendergast*
Agency: *Ketchum Communications*
Client: *Rustoleum*
Category: *Advertising Direct Mail Business*

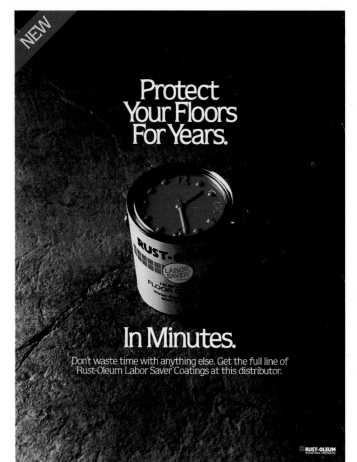

Dimensional
Illustrator: *Christo Holloway*
Art Director: *Roger Bottle*
Photographer: *Nick Tompkin*
Agency: *Creative Connection*
Client: *Cytotec*
Category: *Advertising Illustration*

Dimensional
Illustrator: *Christo Holloway*
Art Director: *Clemb Tholett*
Photographer: *Tony Meintjes*
Agency: *Mundell Tholett*
Client: *Gilbey's*
Category: *Unpublished*

Dimensional
Illustrator: *Christo Holloway*
Art Director: *Derek Hayes*
Photographer: *Nick Tompkin*
Agency: *DMB & B*
Client: *Digital Computers*
Category: *Advertising Illustration*

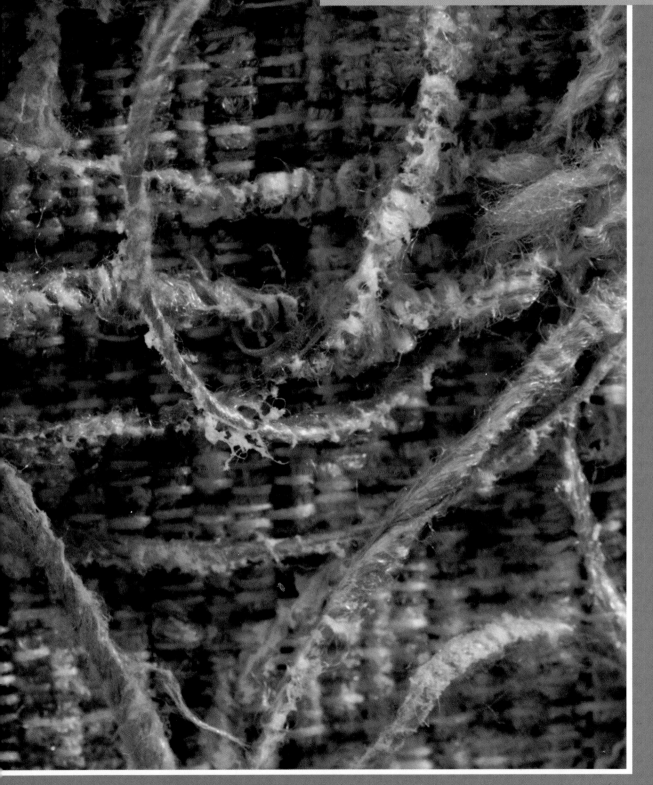

FABRIC SCULPTURE

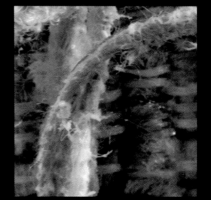

DIMENSIONAL ILLUSTRATIONS CREATED FROM FABRIC ARE IN THE FORM OF FABRIC COLLAGE, SOFT-SCULPTURE AND NEEDLEWORK. THROUGH THE USE OF TEXTURES AND PATTERNS THE FABRIC COLLAGE ARTIST IS ABLE TO REALIZE AN OVERALL TEXTURAL PERSPECTIVE WITHIN A RELATIVELY FLAT PLANE. STUFFED MATERIALS ARE FASHIONED TO CREATE PLIABLE YET PLAYFUL 3-DIMENSIONAL MODELS AND PROPS WHILE NEEDLEWORK AND STITCHERY EMPLOY A NETWORK OF WOVEN COLORED THREADS TO PRODUCE DYNAMIC AND PROVOCATIVE 3-DIMENSIONAL ILLUSTRATIONS. THE APPLICATION OF THESE TECHNIQUES DEMONSTRATES THE VARIETY AND SCOPE OF FABRIC AS A VIABLE 3-DIMENSIONAL MEDIUM FOR THE COMPETITIVE ADVERTISING INDUSTRY.

FABRIC SCULPTURE

"Fabric collage provides the dimensional sculptor a unique textural medium when applied to 3-Dimensional illustration. It gives the illustrator a sculptural versatility of composition within the printed page. This in turn, provides the viewer with an illusionary perspective through the use of patterns and textures. Fabric collage provides an excellent medium for the use of 3-Dimensional design."
ELAINE GOLAK

GOLD AWARD

Spirits & Wines

Piña Colada
Our Pargonian toast to the tropics...with real ice cream!! $3.80

Mai Tai
Mai goodness! One for a high, two for bye-bye. $3.95

Frozen Strawberry Daiquiri
So fresh, it should be slapped. $3.80

Margarita on the Rocks
The gulp of Mexico. That's K-Passa! $3.70

Miss Nubie's Hunchpunch
Miss Nubie's powerful recipe from Panama City.
Reminiscent of....the Hunchpunch Bunch can't remember. $3.70

Pargo's Cafe
The ultimate Pargonian warmer-upper. Just like Myrna...
warm & wonderful. $3.95

Wines for the Times
Red; White or Blush...by the glass
House.............$2.75
Featured.........$3.45

FunFood

Soup or Chowder
Homemade daily. Go on, ask about it. Ask!

Buffalo Wings
With celery sticks and bleu cheese. Bet ya didn't know
there were spicy wings on a buffalo. Wonder if they migrate... $4.25

Mot-Sa-Rel-La Cheese Stix
If you can say it, you can eat it. Served with Italian
marinara sauce. $3.95

Potato Skins
Undoubtably potato-ee. With real bacon and melted cheese.
Tatziki sauce for skinny dipping. $4.95

Pargo's Chili
Mild...but still wild! Served in an incredible edible bowl.
With shredded cheese, onions and tostado chips. $3.75

Mucho Nachos
A Mexican orgy of chili, refried beans, jalapeño peppers and
lotsa melted cheese. With a tease of guacamole and sour
cream. Salsa on the side. Ole'! $5.25

Bite-Size Shrimp
Yet more proof that size isn't everything. A generous portion.
Served with cocktail sauce and frygos. $5.25

Chicken Fingers
From the same joker who brought us buffalo wings. Breaded
tenderloin of chicken breast. Served with our great dipping sauce
and frygos. Myrna gets them confused with chicken *lips*. $5.25

This & That

Bubble Bread Basket
Pargonian style French cheese bread. After all, the French
do it like nobody else. $2.25

Frygos
Lightly seasoned curly fries that go with absolutely
everything. Try a basket full. $1.75

Baked Potato
A spud lover's delight. Available only after 5 p.m. $1.85

Diced Spiced Fruit
A variety of chilled fruits. We diced 'em, then spiced 'em in
orange curacao. Now idn't that healthy? $1.75

Ralph, Myron and Dave. They're really glad to meet ya. Been in sales all their lives–cars, condos, cemetery lots, U-name-it. Known as the Hunchpunch Lunch Bunch. Meet at Pargo's every after-noon. After all, life is short.

George and Edna. Pargo's regulars ever since they tried their first spicy buffalo wings with bleu cheese–always a great way to road test George's newest set of choppers. Eat so many they often skip dinner and go straight for the carrot cake. Edna known to try Mucho Nachos from time to time, especially on bingo night. Says it brings her luck.

Dimensional
Illustrators: *Jan Chalmers/Margaret Cusack*
Art Directors: *S.A. Habib/Steve Hagewood*
Photographer: *David Bailey*
Agency: *Buntin Advertising, Inc.*
Client: *Shoney's Inc. Speciality Restaurant Division*
Category: *Menu*

Dimensional
Illustrator: *Vickey Elsom*
Art Director: *Lynn Ridley*
Photographer: *Ray Boudreau*
Agency: *Kelley Advertising, Inc.*
Client: *Dow Chemical Canada, Inc.*
Category: *Advertising Illustration*
        Advertising Direct Mail Business Poster

Dimensional
Illustrator: *Mary M. Bono*
Art Director: *Doug Steinbauer*
Photographer: *Mary M. Bono*
Publisher: *Whitney Publications*
Client: *5O Plus Magazine*
Category: *Editorial Magazine Full Page*

Fabric Illustration

Ann Morton Hubbard

Dimensional
Illustrator: *Ann Morton Hubbard*
Art Director: *Ann Morton Hubbard*
Photographer: *Tony Hernandez*
Agency: *Hubbard & Hubbard Design*
Publisher: *The Arizona Portfolio*
Client: *The Arizona Portfolio*
Category: *Self Promotion*

Dimensional
Illustrator: *Margaret Cusack*
Art Director: *Cynthia Magalian*
Photographer: *Ron Breland*
Publisher: *Macy's*
Client: *Macy's*
Category: *Advertising Direct Mail Poster*

S I L V E R

A W A R D

Dimensional
Illustrator: *Margaret Cusack*
Art Director: *Rubin Pfeiffer*
Photographer: *Ron Breland*
Publisher: *Harcourt Brace Jovanovich*
Client: *Greene Cross*
Category: *Greeting Card*

Dimensional
Illustrator: *Margaret Cusack*
Art Director: *Ralph Kellner*
Photographer: *Ron Breland*
Agency: *Kellner & Osburn*
Client: *Fulton Street Mall Improvement Association*
Category: *Illustration Advertising Billboard*

Dimensional
Illustrator: *Jerry Pavey*
Art Director: *Lucy Bartholomew*
Agency: *The Publishing Group*
Publisher: *Bell Atlantic*
Client: *C & P Telephone/Bell Atlantic*
Category: *Magazine Editorial Consumer Campaign*

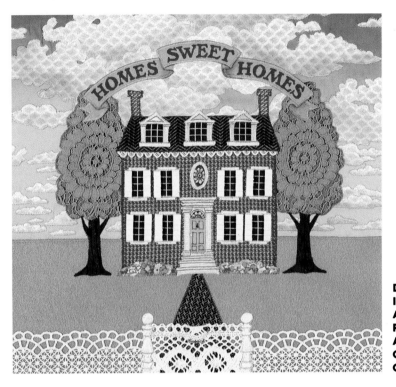

Dimensional
Illustrator: *Margaret Cusack*
Art Director: *Jo Bertone*
Photographer: *Ron Breland*
Agency: *Penny & Speier*
Client: *Greater Houston Builders*
Category: *Magazine Advertising Full Page*

Dimensional
Illustrator: *Margaret Cusack*
Art Director: *Bill Santry*
Photographer: *Jim Noble*
Agency: *Earle Palmer Brown, Bethesda*
Client: *Freddie Mac, Federal Home Loan Mortgage Corporation*
Category: *Advertising Direct Mail Poster*

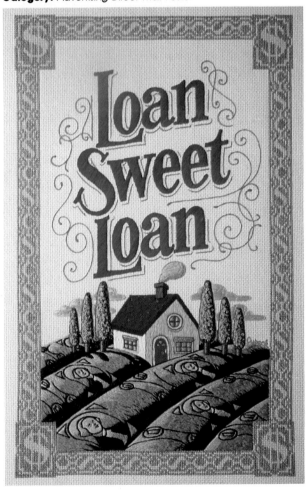

Dimensional
Illustrator: *Margaret Cusack*
Art Director: *Richard Loretoni*
Photographer: *Ron Breland*
Publisher: *Gruner & Jahr USA Publishing*
Client: *Parents Magazine*
Category: *Editorial Magazine Consumer*

Dimensional
Illustrator: Margaret Cusack
Art Director: Tom Rosenfield
Photographer: Ron Breland
Agency: DDB Needham
Client: Seagram's
Category: Magazine Advertising Full Page

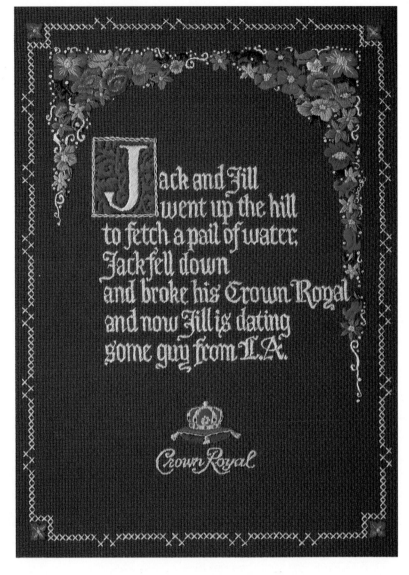

Dimensional
Illustrator: Kathy Lengyel
Art Director: Richard Webb
Photographer: Mike Moakler
Agency: Mackowski & Company
Client: YKK Zippers
Category: Unpublished

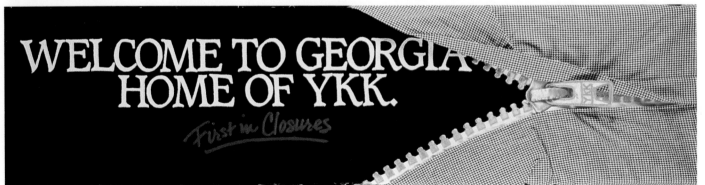

Dimensional
Illustrator: *Ann Morton Hubbard*
Art Director: *Rosemary Connelly*
Photographer: *Bill Timmerman*
Agency: *Richardson or Richardson*
Publisher: *The Arizona Portfolio*
Client: *Digi Type*
Category: *Magazine Advertising Full Page*

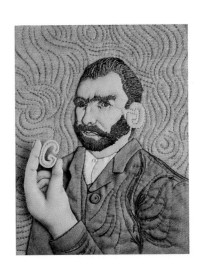

Number Two in a Series.

GREAT TYPEFACES

We set characters for characters with character at
3118 North 7th Avenue, Phoenix, Arizona
602-264-2425

© 1987 DigiType. Fabric Illustration Ann Morton Hubbard.

Dimensional
Illustrator: *Kathy Lengyel*
Art Director: *Kathy Lengyel*
Photographer: *John Siebenthaler*
Client: *Morton Plant Hospital*
Category: *Advertising Direct Mail Brochure*

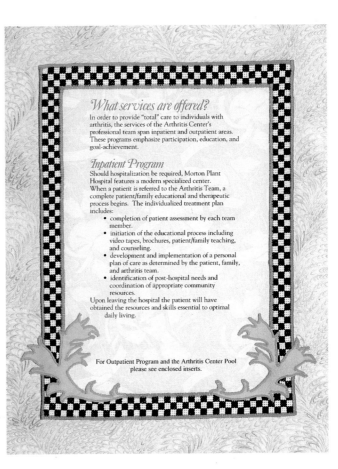

Dimensional
Illustrator: *Margaret Cusack*
Art Director: *Charles Edmondson*
Photographer: *Skip Caplan*
Agency: *E. James White Company*
Publisher: *Charles Keath, Ltd.*
Category: *Advertising Illustration*

Dimensional
Illustrator: *Jerry Pavey*
Art Director: *Jerry Pavey*
Photographer: *Tom Radcliffe*
Agency: *Jerry Pavey Design & Illustration*
Publisher: *Svec/Conway Printing*
Client: *Farm Credit Banks Funding Corporation*
Category: *Editorial Illustration*

Dimensional
Illustrator: *Margaret Cusack*
Art Director: *Ross Sutherland*
Photographer: *Skip Caplan*
Agency: *Ogilvy & Mather*
Client: *Kraft General Foods*
Category: *Illustration Advertising*

Dimensional
Illustrator: *Margaret Cusack*
Art Director: *Steve Snyder*
Photographer: *Skip Caplan*
Publisher: *Little Brown & Co.*
Client: *Little Brown & Co.*
Category: *Book Cover*

Dimensional
Illustrator: *Margaret Cusack*
Art Director *Martha Linton*
Photographer: *Ron Breland*
Agency: *Home Mission Board*
Category: *Advertising Direct Mail Poster*

Dimensional
Illustrator: *Jerry Pavey*
Art Director: *Jerry Pavey*
Photographer: *Tom Radcliffe*
Agency: *Jerry Pavey Design & Illustration*
Publisher: *S & S Graphics, Inc.*
Client: *S.D. Warren Paper Co./S & S Graphics,Inc.*
Category: *Editorial Illustration*

Dimensional
Illustrator: *Bonnie J. Lallky*
Photographer: *Carl Seibert*
Publisher: *News/Sun Sentinel*
Category: *Unpublished*

Dimensional
Illustrator: *Bonnie J. Lallky*
Art Director: *Kathy Hensley Trumbull*
Photographer: *Rich Mahan*
Publisher: *News/Sun-Sentinel*
Category: *Newspaper*

Dimensional
Illustrator: *Deanna Glad*
Art Director: *Chris Mossman*
Publisher: *East/West Network*
Client: *Mainliner*
Category: *Editorial Illustration*

Dimensional
Illustrator: *Kathy Lengyel*
Art Director: *Steve Justice*
Photographer: *Paul Kluber*
Publisher: *Dynamics Graphics, Inc.*
Category: *Advertising Illustration*

Dimensional
Illustrator: *Deanna Glad*
Photographer: *David Ives*
Designer: *Don Dame*
Publisher: *Windemere Press*
Category: *Self Promotion*

WOOD SCULPTURE

THE INHERENT TEXTURE OF WOOD MAKES THIS MEDIUM AN IDEAL CHOICE FOR 3-DIMENSIONAL ILLUSTRATIONS. WHEN STAINED OR VARNISHED, THE NATURAL POROUS SURFACE SERVES TO DEMONSTRATE THE OVERALL BEAUTY OF MODELS FABRICATED FROM WOOD. TECHNIQUES RANGING FROM LOW RELIEF CARVINGS TO FREE-STANDING SCULPTURES ACCENTUATE THE BOUNDLESS SHAPES, DESIGNS AND APPLICATIONS OF THIS MOST VERSATILE FIBROUS MATERIAL. THE INTRINSIC GRAIN PATTERNS AND SUBTLE TONAL VARIATIONS DEMONSTRATE THE MULTIFACETED ASPECTS OF WOOD AS A UNIQUELY ADAPTABLE SOLUTION FOR THE CONTEMPORARY ADVERTISING INDUSTRY.

WOOD SCULPTURE

"When executed with real vision, dimensional illustration can be visibly a lot more appealing than its flatmate. It adds another dimension of possibility to an idea."
PETER HOBDEN

NOW WOOD
DOESN'T
HAVE TO BE
SO WOODEN.

Oak, Ash, Beech, Walnut,
Sycamore, Maple, Pine.
Wood, whatever the species,
has a warmth and beauty
all of its own.
Wood has a colour all its
own too. Brown.
Any attempt to change
that usually involves coat-
ing it with paint or stripping
it with bleach.
Thankfully
there is now
an alternative
treatment.
New Dulux Woodtones. A
low sheen finish that changes a
wood's colour, yet allows the
character and feel of its grain
to shine through.
There are nine varieties.
From green to grey, peach to
pale blue.
In just two light coats
you'll have a hard wearing
surface on anything wooden.
From the window frames
to the picture frames. From
the side board to the floor
boards.
And should you be
that way inclined, the
'apples and pears.'

Dulux
WOODTONES

Dimensional
Illustrator: *Matthew Wurr*
Art Director: *Mike Durban*
Photographer: *Graham Ford*
Agency: *WCRS*
Client: *Dulux Wood Paint*
Category: *Magazine Advertising Spread*

Dimensional
Illustrator: *Bonnie Rasmussen*
Designer: *Lee Arters*
Photographer: *Sauer & Associates*
Agency: *Slater-Hanft-Martin-(NYC)*
Client: *Thompson & Formby*
Category: *Unpublished*

Dimensional
Illustrator: *Nancy Blauers*
Photographer: *Maurice Sherman*
Category: *Unpublished*

Dimensional
Illustrator: *Bill Schmeelk*
Art Director: *Thomas Darnsteadt*
Photographer: *Ken Schroers*
Agency: *Medical Economics Company*
Publisher: *Bill Reynolds*
Client: *Drug Topics Magazine*
Category: *Editorial Magazine Business Cover*

Dimensional
Illustrator: *Peter Buchman*
Art Director: *Kristina Perry*
Photographer: *Big City*
Agency: *Grey Advertising*
Client: *Madison Square Garden Network*
Category: *Advertising Direct Mail Brochure*

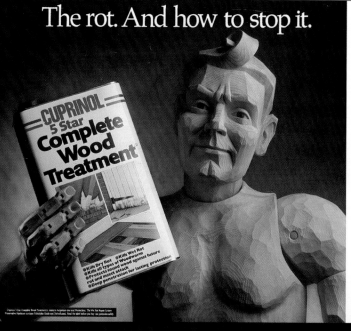

The rot. And how to stop it.

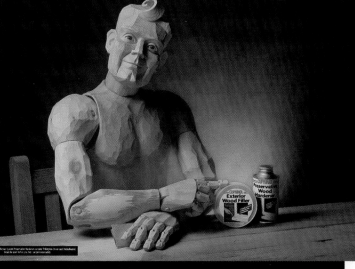

The new Cuprinol Wet Rot Repair System.
It could save you an arm and a leg.

Cuprinol Wood Preserver penetrates
up to ten times more than others.

Dimensional
Illustrator: *Matthew Wurr*
Art Director: *Chris Hodgkiss*
Photographer: *Jerry Oke*
Agency: *Cogent Elliott*
Client: *Cuprinol Wood Treatments*
Category: *Magazine Advertising Consumer
       Campaign*

Dimensional
Illustrator: *James Nazz*
Photographer: *Victor Sartor*
Category: *Self Promotion*

Dimensional
Illustrator: *Mary Lynn Coleman*
Publisher: *Hallmark Cards, Inc.*
Category: *Greeting Card*

Dimensional
Illustrator: *Mary Lynn Coleman*
Publisher: *Hallmark Cards, Inc.*
Category: *Greeting Card*

Dimensional
Illustrator: *Mary Lynn Coleman*
Publisher: *Hallmark Cards, Inc.*
Category: *Greeting Card*

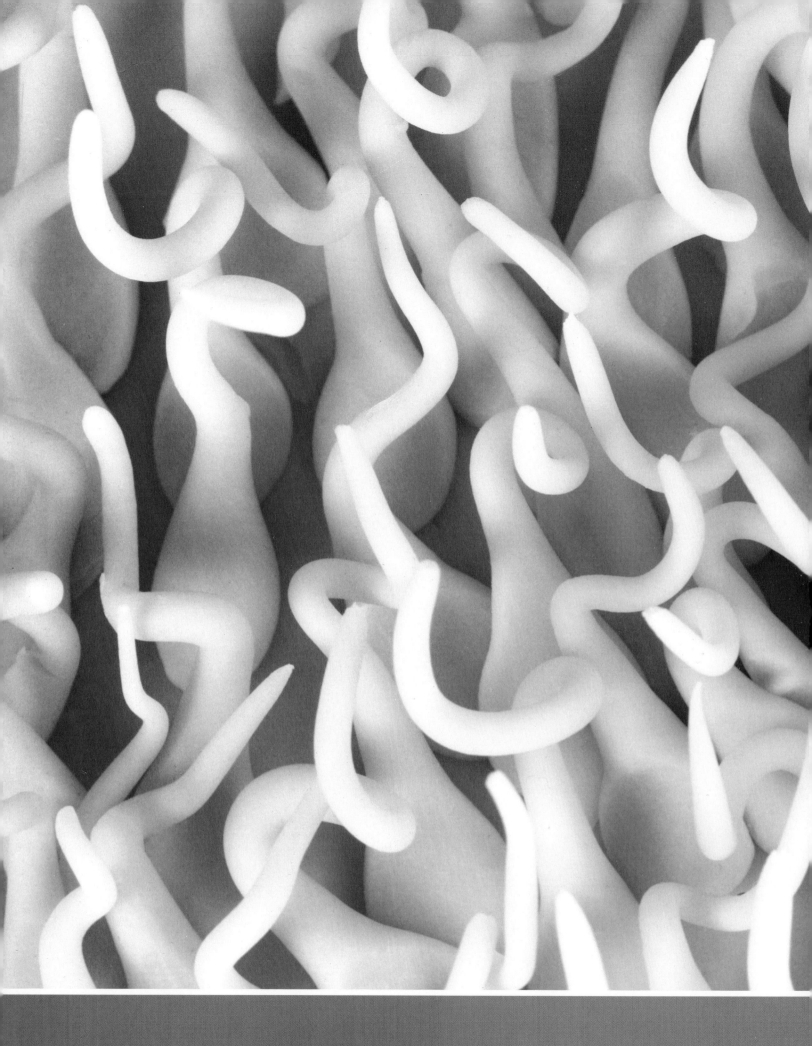

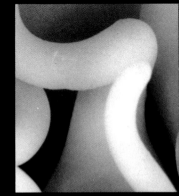

CLAY SCULPTURE

CLAY AFFORDS THE SCULPTOR THE FREEDOM AND FLEXIBILITY TO CREATE MODELS THAT UTILIZE A LIMITLESS RADIUS OF DESIGN. THE PLIABILITY OF PLASTILINA AND CERAMIC CLAY OFFER AN UNRESTRICTED CREATIVE LICENSE OF SHAPES AND IMAGES WHICH WOULD BE DIFFICULT FOR THE 2-DIMENSIONAL RENDERER. MODERN CLAY ANIMATION TECHNIQUES ALSO PROVIDE A PLAYFUL YET METICULOUS AVENUE IN WHICH TO EXAMINE THE FOURTH-DIMENSION OF IL-LUSTRATIVE MOVEMENT THROUGH SPACE AND TIME. AS AN ADVERTISING MEDIUM, CLAY SCULPTURE CONTINUES TO ENJOY A LARGE POR-TION OF TODAY'S DIMENSIONAL ILLUSTRATION MARKET.

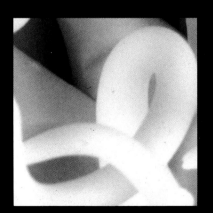

"I look forward to the day when Claymation® becomes very widely accepted as an entertainment medium, just like traditional cel animation. I've often said that if Walt Disney had been a sculptor instead of a graphic artist, maybe things would have flip-flopped. Three-dimensional illustration is naturally a more human or intimate way of illustrating - it's the way people see. For me the marriage of sculptural forms and stop-motion animation is incredibly satisfying, both in the creation and in the final product."

WILL VINTON

GOLD

AWARD

Dimensional
Illustrator: *Shelley Daniels*
Art Director: *Barry Simon*
Photographer: *Michael Marzelli*
Publisher: *PSC Publications*
Client: *Games Special Edition*
Category: *Magazine Editorial Consumer Cover*

Dimensional
Illustrators: *Lee & Mary Sievers*
Art Director: *Lee Sievers*
Photographer: *Rod Pierce*
Agency: *Sievers' Studio*
Publisher: *Meadow Creek Gallery*
Category: *Unpublished*

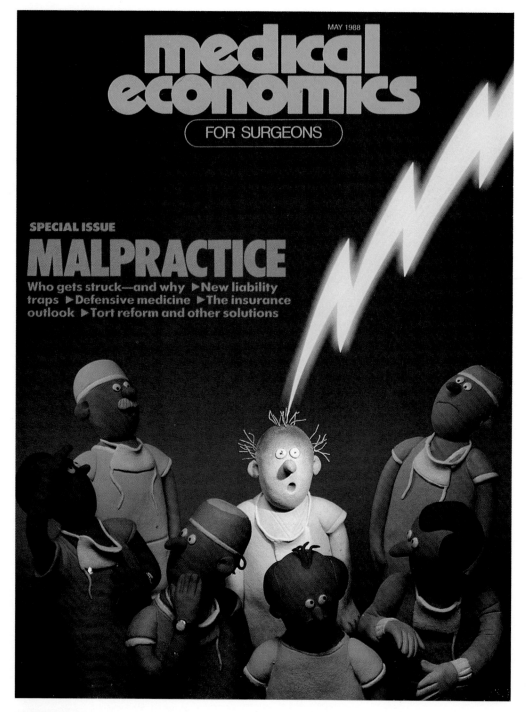

Dimensional
Illustrator: *Gordon Swenarton*
Art Director: *William Kuhn*
Photographer: *Stephen Munz*
Agency: *Medical Economics Company*
Publisher: *Jim Jenkins*
Client: *Medical Economics for Surgeons*
Category: *Editorial Magazine Business Cover*

Dimensional
Illustrator: *Robert Chatwin*
Art Director: *Jonathan Rogers*
Photographer: *Peter Hogan*
Agency: *Peter Hogan Associates*
Publisher: *Professional Publishing Asso.*
Client: *Great Expectations Magazine*
Category: *Magazine Editorial Consumer Cover*

SILVER

AWARD

YOUR HOSPITAL IS LOOKING OUT FOR NO. 1

Now that their own malpractice risks have increased, hospitals are relentlessly tightening their grip on physicians.

By Mark Crane SENIOR EDITOR

HOW MUCH MALPRACTICE CAN BE BLAMED ON BAD DOCTORS?

There may be 40,000 doctors who are unfit to practice. Getting rid of them won't be easy and may not relieve the malpractice crisis.

By M. Carroll Thomas MIDWEST EDITOR

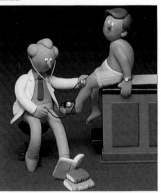

APRIL 18, 1988

medical economics

SPECIAL ISSUE

MALPRACTICE

WHY 6 OF 10 DOCTORS FACE CLAIMS

WHERE NEW LIABILITY TRAPS LIE

DOES DEFENSIVE MEDICINE REALLY WORK?

THE OUTLOOK ON INSURANCE

CAN TORT REFORM SAVE THE DAY?

SOLUTIONS THAT SHOW PROMISE

DEEPER TROUBLE AHEAD FOR THE JOINT-RISK POOLS

To keep these "insurers of last resort" from going broke, every doctor may need to pay higher premiums for malpractice coverage.

By Mark Crane SENIOR EDITOR

Dimensional
Illustrator: *Gordon Swenarton*
Art Director: *Roger Dowd*
Photographer: *Stephen Munz*
Agency: *Medical Economics Company*
Publisher: *Jim Jenkins*
Client: *Medical Economics Magazine*
Category: *Editorial Magazine Business Campaign*

SILVER AWARD

Dimensional
Illustrator: *Timothy Young*
Art Director: *Gary Blake*
Photographer: *Bruno*
Agency: *Siebel/Mohr Inc.*
Client: *Leroux Liquors*
Category: *Point Of Purchase Display Campaign*

Dimensional
Illustrator: *Gordon Swenarton*
Art Director: *Larry Stiers*
Photographer: *John F. Cooper*
Agency: *Ciba Geigy*
Client: *Ciba Geigy*
Category: *Advertising Magazine Full Page*

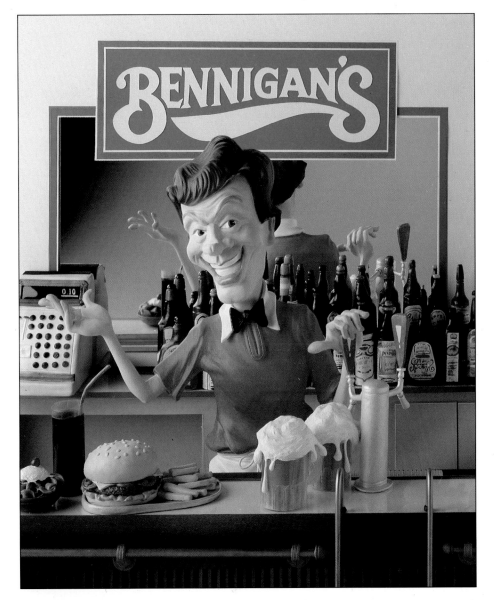

Dimensional
Illustrator: *Jack Graham*
Art Director: *Jack Graham*
Photographer: *Bob Carey*
Category: *Advertising Illustration*

Dimensional
Illustrator: *Richard McNeel*
Art Director: *Peter Miller*
Photographer: *William G. Wagner*
Agency: *Compugraphic Corporation*
Client: *Compugraphic Corporation*
Category: *Calendar*

Dimensional
Illustrator: *Jack Graham*
Art Director: *Jack Graham*
Photographer: *Bob Carey*
Category: *Editorial Illustration*

Dimensional
Illustrator: *Kathy Jeffers*
Art Director: *Jack Frakes*
Agency: *Ross Roy Advertising*
Client: *K Mart*
Category: *Advertising Magazine Consumer*

Dimensional
Illustrator: *Sue Carey*
Photographer: *Bill Carey*
Category: *Unpublished*

Dimensional
Illustrator: *Richard McNeel*
Art Director: *Ron Meyerson*
Photographer: *William G. Wagner*
Publisher: *Newsweek Magazine*
Category: *Editorial Magazine Consumer Cover*

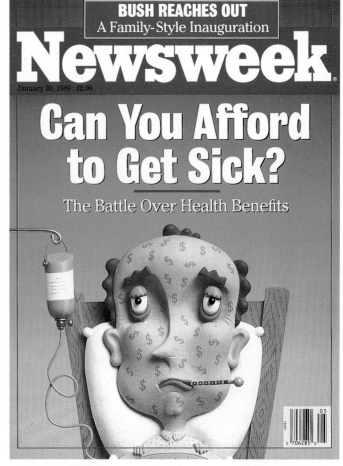

Dimensional
Illustrator: *Gordon Swenarton*
Art Directors: *Thomas Darnsteadt/John Newcomb*
Photographer: *Stephen Munz*
Agency: *Medical Economics Company*
Publisher: *Bill Reynolds*
Client: *Drug Topics Magazine*
Category: *Editorial Magazine Business Cover*

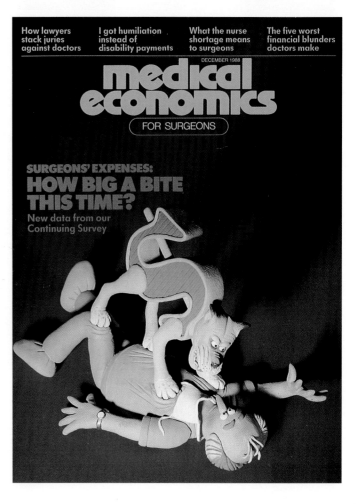

Dimensional
Illustrator: *Gordon Swenarton*
Art Director: *William Kuhn*
Photographer: *Stephen Munz*
Agency: *Medical Economics Company*
Publisher: *Jim Jenkins*
Client: *Medical Economics for Surgeons*
Category: *Editorial Magazine Business Cover*

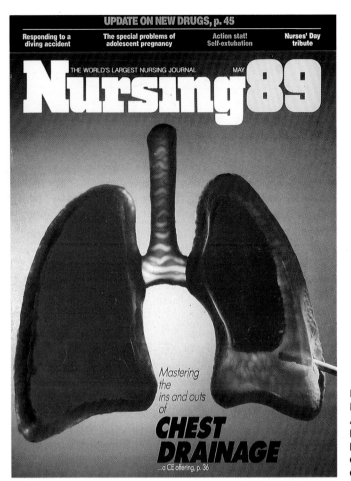

M E R I T

A W A R D S

Dimensional
Illustrator: *Kathleen Ziegler*
Art Director: *Jake Smith*
Photographer: *Bob Emmott*
Publisher: *Springhouse Corporation*
Client: *Nursing '89*
Category: *Magazine Editorial Business Cover*

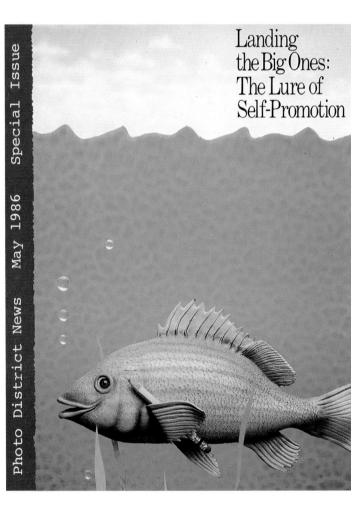

Dimensional
Illustrator: *James Nazz*
Art Director: *Peter Ross*
Photographer: *James Nazz*
Category: *Editorial Magazine Consumer Cover*

Dimensional
Illustrator: *Gordon Swenarton*
Art Director: *Roger Dowd*
Photographer: *Stephen E. Munz*
Agency: *Falcone & Associates*
Publisher: *Medical Economics Company, Inc.*
Client: *Medical Economics*
Category: *Editorial Magazine Business Cover*

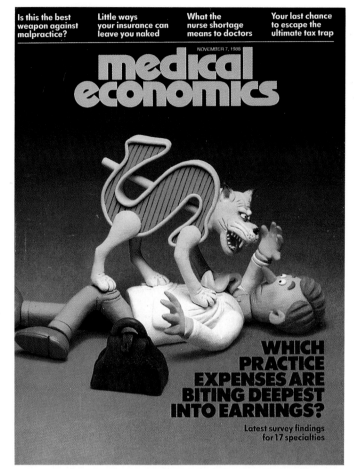

Dimensional
Illustrator: *Ardith Truhan*
Art Director: *Stephen Wierzbicki*
Photographer: *Bill Wagner*
Publisher: *Times Mirror Magazines*
Client: *Ski Magazine*
Category: *Editorial Magazine Consumer Spread*

Dimensional
Illustrator: *Kathy Jeffers*
Art Director: *Ken Surabian*
Photographer: *Chris Vincent*
Publisher: *Bill Communications*
Client: *Sales & Marketing Management Magazine*
Category: *Editorial Magazine Business*

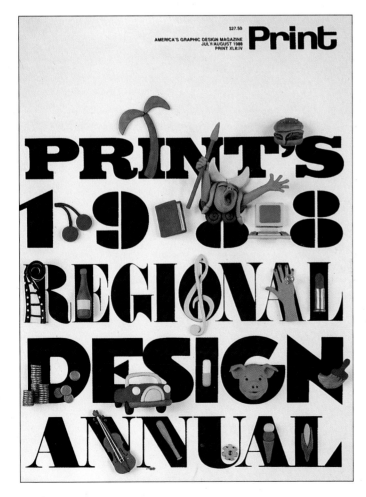

Dimensional
Illustrator: *Shelley Daniels*
Art Director: *Andrew Kner*
Photographer: *Galante/Marzelli*
Publisher: *RC Publications*
Client: *Print Magazine*
Category: *Editorial Magazine Business Cover*

Dimensional
Illustrator: *Bonnie J. Lallky*
Art Director: *George Benge*
Photographer: *John Curry*
Publisher: *SND Design Magazine*
Category: *Newspaper*

Dimensional
Illustrator: *Kathy Jeffers*
Art Director: *Ken Surabian*
Photographer: *Chris Vincent*
Publisher: *Bill Communications*
Client: *Sales & Marketing Management Magazine*
Category: *Editorial Magazine Business Spread*

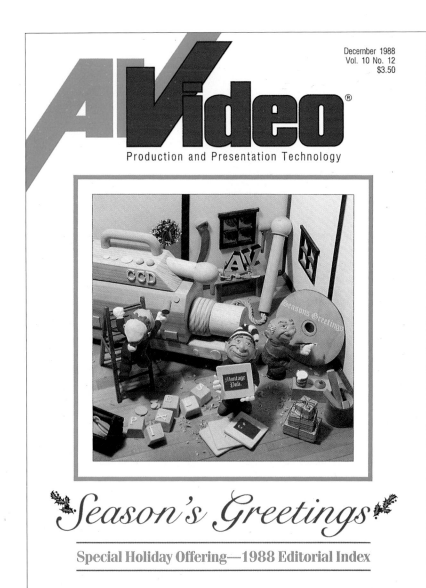

December 1988
Vol. 10 No. 12
$3.50

AVideo ®

Production and Presentation Technology

Season's Greetings

Special Holiday Offering—1988 Editorial Index

Dimensional
Illustrator: *Bob Schuchman*
Art Director: *Peter Chaffey*
Photographer: *Bob Schuchman*
Publisher: *Montage Publishing*
Client: *AV Video*
Category: *Editorial Magazine Business Campaign*

I'm dreaming of a slide Christmas.
Just like the ones I used to know.
Where projectors glistened,
And clients listened,
Before they heard of video.

I'm dreaming of a slide Christmas.
With every rough draft that I write.
May your charts be colored and bright.
And may all your overheads be spelled right.

I heard the bells
On DAT today.
Their brilliance blew
My mind away.

How loud and sweet.
Those sounds repeat.
Will good men keep
The market gray.

Hal—lelujah.
Vec—tored graphic.
Bit-mapped magic.
With ray-tracing.
Hal—le—lu—jah.

Scan—ner Input.
Pre—Press Output.
Desktop printing.
Is MAC winning?
Hal—le—lu—jah.

Dimensional
Illustrator: *Bonnie J. Lallky*
Art Director: *Kent Barton*
Photographer: *Nick Von Staden*
Publisher: *Sunshine Magazine*
Category: *Newspaper*

Dimensional
Illustrator: *Andrea Arroyo*
Art Director: *Jim Russek*
Photographer: *Ralph Masullo*
Agency: *Russek Advertising*
Client: *The Joyce Theater*
Category: *Illustration Advertising*

Dimensional
Illustrator: *Bonnie J. Lallky*
Photographer: *John Curry*
Publisher: *News/Sun-Sentinel*
Category: *Newspaper*

Dimensional
Illustrator: *Bonnie J. Lallky*
Photographer: *John Curry*
Publisher: *News/Sun-Sentinel*
Category: *Newspaper*

Dimensional
Illustrator: *Richard McNeel*
Art Director: *Art Jones*
Photographer: *William G. Wagner*
Agency: *Brannigan DeMarco Communications, NY*
Client: *Alupent/Boehringer Ingelheim Pharmaceuticals Inc.*
Category: *Advertising Direct Mail Brochure*

Dimensional
Illustrator: *Kathy Jeffers*
Art Director: *Kevin Weidenbacher*
Photographer: *Chris Vincent*
Agency: *Scali McCabe Sloves*
Client: *Hertz*
Category: *Advertising Magazine Consumer*

With our guaranteed European rates, you have a choice. Save now or save later.

With Hertz Affordable Europe, you have a choice of two guaranteed rates.
You can pay a rate that's guaranteed in American dollars before you leave for Europe. Or you can pay one that's guaranteed in local currencies when you're there.
Either way, you can be sure the rate you'll be paying is a great value.
Of course, guaranteed rates aren't all that make Hertz Affordable Europe the best choice for vacation travelers. We have a wide variety of cars. And there's all our special services. Like unlimited mileage and our 24-hour Emergency Road Service.
Plus, we have over 1300 locations throughout Europe, each with an English-speaking staff.
All the more reason to call your travel agent or Hertz at 1-800-654-3001. Because at Hertz, we have what it takes to make travelers happy. No matter what side of the Atlantic they're on.

Hertz rents Fords and other fine cars.

Hertz
Affordable Europe

Dimensional
Illustrator: *Andrea Arroyo*
Art Directors: *Susan Hussey/Carol Glass*
Photographer: *Max Chester*
Publisher: *Organica Press*
Client: *Aubrey Organics*
Category: *Newspaper*

Dimensional
Illustrator: *Richard McNeel*
Art Director: *Bill Horner*
Photographer: *William G. Wagner*
Agency: *Busch Creative Services Corporation*
Client: *Budweiser*
Category: *Magazine Advertising Spread*

159

Dimensional
Illustrator: *Marilyn Bass*
Art Director: *Sandy Whitby*
Photographer: *Marvin Goldman*
Agency: *Pitluck*
Client: *Kinetic Concepts*
Category: *Advertising Direct Mail Brochure*

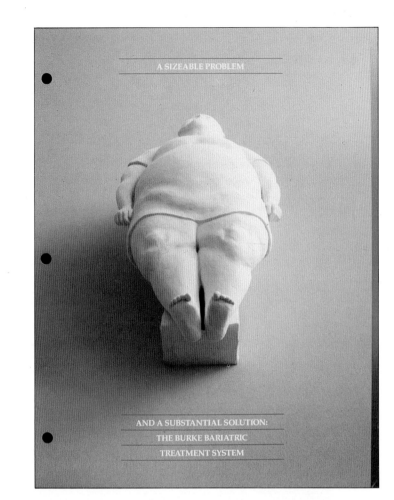

Dimensional
Illustrator: *R. Scott Purcell*
Art Director: *R. Scott Purcell*
Photographer: *Jennifer Barret*
Agency: *Parlor Productions*
Client: *First Pennsylvania Bank*
 Springfield Tricentenial Comm.
Category: *Animated Film Still*

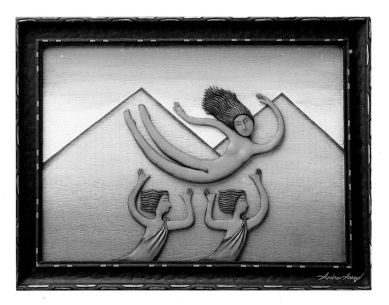

A NEW LEAF AT THE JOYCE

Dimensional
Illustrator: *Andrea Arroyo*
Art Director: *Jim Russek*
Photographer: *Ralph Masullo*
Agency: *Russek Advertising*
Client: *The Joyce Theater*
Category: *Illustration Advertising*

Dimensional
Illustrator: *Gordon Swenarton*
Art Director: *Gordon Swenarton*
Photographer: *Lynn Bodek*
Agency: *Falcone & Associates*
Publisher: *Falcone & Associates*
Client: *Falcone & Associates*
Category: *Self Promotion Poster*

Dimensional
Illustrator: *Jack Graham*
Art Director: *Curtis Carter*
Photographer: *Bob Carey*
Publisher: *George Gretser*
Client: *Private Clubs*
Category: *Editorial Illustration*

Dimensional
Illustrators: *Lee & Mary Sievers*
Art Director: *Lee Sievers*
Photographer: *Tom Nelson*
Agency: *Sievers' Studio*
Client: *The Marks Gallery*
Category: *Unpublished*

Dimensional
Illustrator: *Jef Workman*
Art Director: *Jef Workman*
Photographer: *Mark Rice*
Agency: *Bird In The Hand Studio*
Client: *Bird In The Hand Studio*
Category: *Unpublished*

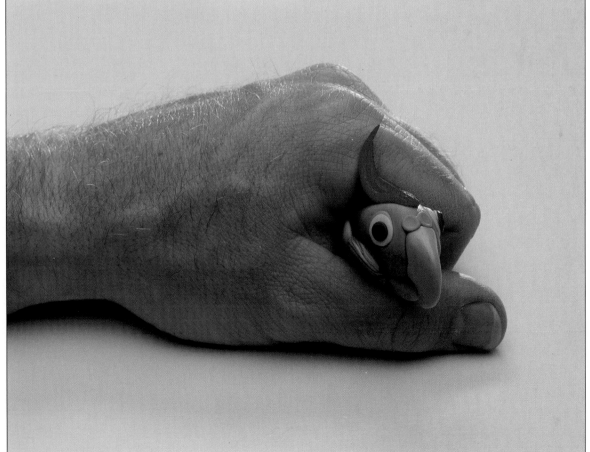

Dimensional
Illustrator: *Sheila Quick*
Art Director: *Sheila Quick*
Photographer: *Hessel Algera*
Category: *Unpublished*

Dimensional
Illustrator: *Sol Rothman*
Art Director: *Sol Rothman*
Photographer: *Chris Murray*
Agency: *Rothman Studios*
Category: *Unpublished*

On your birthday, party till the sheep come home!

Meet my neighbor, Pete. Pete's a very, very lonely guy. Y'know the type--never had a date in high school, went to his senior prom with his sister.

Pete lives with his guppy. He's incredibly shy and doesn't go out much. It's sad, but the highlight of his day is seeing what I get in my evening mail!

So please write...

A co-worker like you comes along once every 1,000 years...

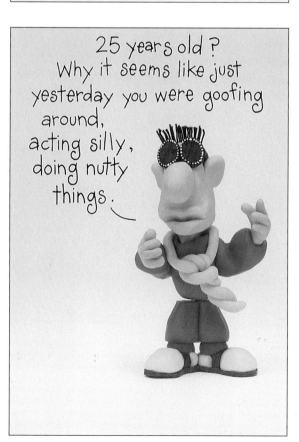

25 years old? Why it seems like just yesterday you were goofing around, acting silly, doing nutty things.

Dimensional
Illustrator: *Mike Willard*
Art Director: *John Ball*
Agency: *Shoebox Greetings*
Publisher: *Hallmark Cards, Inc.*
Client: *Shoebox Greetings*
Category: *Greeting Card*

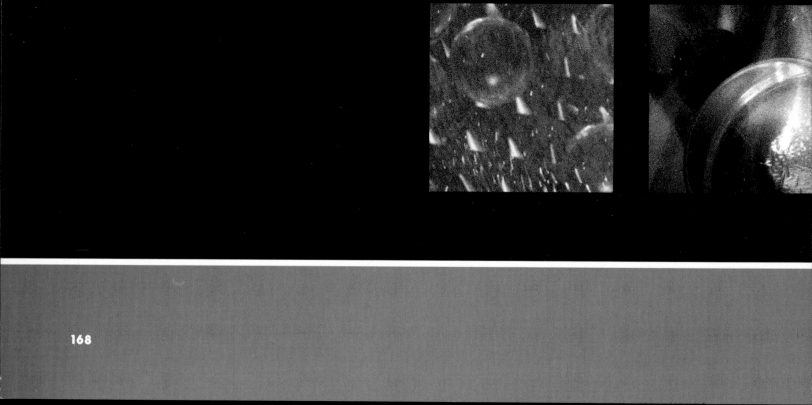

MIXED MEDIA ARTISTRY SPANS THE CREATIVE GAMUT OF 3-DIMENSIONAL MODELMAKING AND DESIGN. THESE MULTITALENTED PRACTITIONERS MUST BE SKILLED IN ALL MEDIA IN ORDER TO CREATE MODELS WHICH POSSESS THE BALANCE AND HARMONY NECESSARY TO CREATE VISUALLY STIMULATING ILLUSTRATIONS. THE ABILITY TO BLEND FOUND OBJECTS, SCULPTURAL ASSEM-BLAGE AND MODELMAKING, DEMANDS A COM-PLETE MASTERY OF 3-DIMENSIONAL DESIGN TECHNIQUES. THE FREEDOM TO EXPLORE ALL FACETS OF THE INDUSTRY OFFERS THE MIXED MEDIA ARTIST AN OPPORTUNITY TO CREATE MULTIFACETED ILLUSTRATIONS WHICH CAP-TIVATE THE IMAGINATION AND COMMAND THE INTEREST OF THE VIEWER.

"Any illustration should convey something to the reader. Three-dimensional illustration takes the number of decisions that lead up to a finished piece and multiplies them in complexity. Illustrations can be built out of anything, wood, paper, twine or plastic. When I look at a three-dimensional piece of art all the problems of the creation of a piece should not be apparent. Instead, one should arrive at the feeling of the style of the artist and a sense of what the artist was trying to communicate. The fact that the piece is three-dimensional should only bring more to what it means and what it is trying to say. After all, the artist has had the benefits of a larger palette out of which he can fashion his art."
MEREDITH HAMILTON

GOLD

AWARD

Dimensional
Illustrator: *Carl Tese*
Art Director: *Ron Meyerson*
Photographer: *George Hausman*
Agency: *Newsweek*
Publisher: *Newsweek*
Client: *Newsweek*
Category: *Magazine Editorial Consumer Cover*

Dimensional
Illustrator: *Jim Victor*
Art Director: *Norm Schaefer*
Photographer: *Kelvin McGowen*
Publisher: *Philadelphia Inquirer*
Category: *Newspaper*

GOLD
AWARD

Dimensional
Illustrators: *Joan Steiner/Irene Pombo*
Art Director: *William Kuhn*
Photographer: *Stephen Munz*
Agency: *Medical Economics Company*
Publisher: *Jim Jenkins*
Client: *Medical Economics for Surgeons*
Category: *Editorial Magazine Business Cover*

Dimensional
Illustrator: *Prop Art McConnell & Borow, Inc.*
Art Director: *Tom McManus*
Photographer: *Steve Bronstein*
Agency: *TBWA*
Client: *Absolut Vodka*
Category: *Magazine Advertising Full Page*

GOLD
AWARD

The pictures by ACHIM KIEL on the theme BREWING and TECHNIQUE for the brewery Feldschlößchen AG in Braunschweig/West Germany, a member of the HOLSTEN group.

Dimensional
Illustrator: *Achim Kiel*
Art Director: *Dirk Wegener*
Photographer: *Uwe Brandes*
Agency: *Pencil Corporate Art*
Publisher: *Pencil Art Edition*
Client: *Brewery Feldschlobchen AG/ Holsten Group*
Category: *Advertising Direct Mail Consumer*

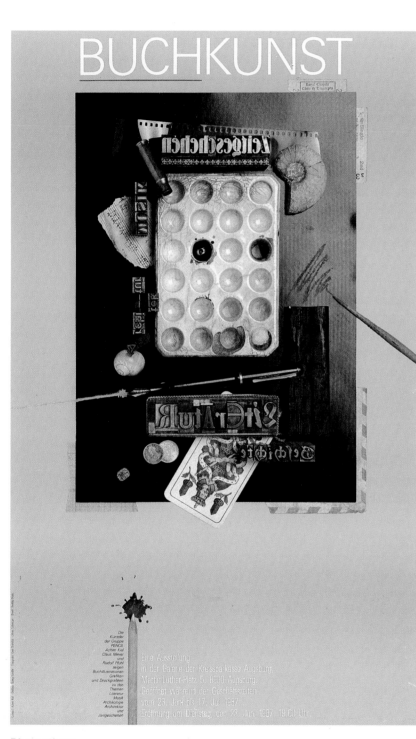

Dimensional
Illustrator: *Achim Kiel*
Art Director: *Achim Kiel*
Photographer: *Uwe Brandes*
Agency: *Pencil Corporate Art*
Publisher: *Pencil Art Editions*
Client: *The National Exhibition Of Book-Art*
Category: *Advertising Direct Mail Consumer*

GOLD

AWARD

Dimensional
Illustrator: *Douglas Watson*
Art Director: *Douglas Watson*
Photographer: *Douglas McBride*
Client: *Reader's Digest Young Illustrators*
Category: *Editorial Illustration*

Dimensional
Illustrator: *Joan Kritchman Knuteson*
Art Director: *Robert Send*
Photographer: *Allen Knox Studio*
Agency: *Scott Advertising*
Client: *O. Mustadt & Sons, Inc.*
Category: *Advertising Illustration*

GOLD AWARD

Dimensional
Illustrator: *Prop Art McConnell & Borow, Inc.*
Art Director: *Tony Santos*
Photographer: *Steve Bronstein*
Agency: *Bozell, Jacobs, Kenyon & Eckhart*
Client: *American International Group*
Category: *Unpublished*

Dimensional
Illustrator: *Prop Art McConnell & Borow, Inc.*
Art Director: *Glen Scheur*
Photographer: *Steve Bronstein*
Agency: *Smith-Greenland*
Client: *Johnny Walker Black Label Scotch Whisky*
Category: *Magazine Advertising Full Page*

SILVER AWARD

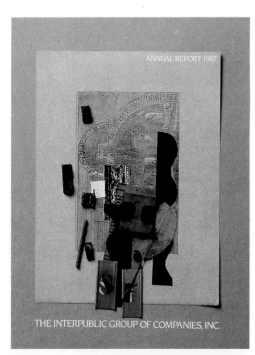

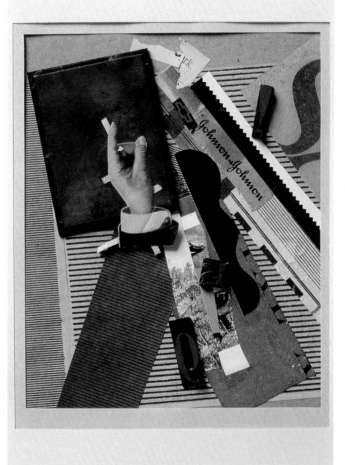

Dimensional
Illustrator: *Fred Otnes*
Art Director: *H.L. VanderBerg*
Agency: *Lowe Marschalk Design Group*
Client: *The Interpublic Group of Companies*
Category: *Annual Report*

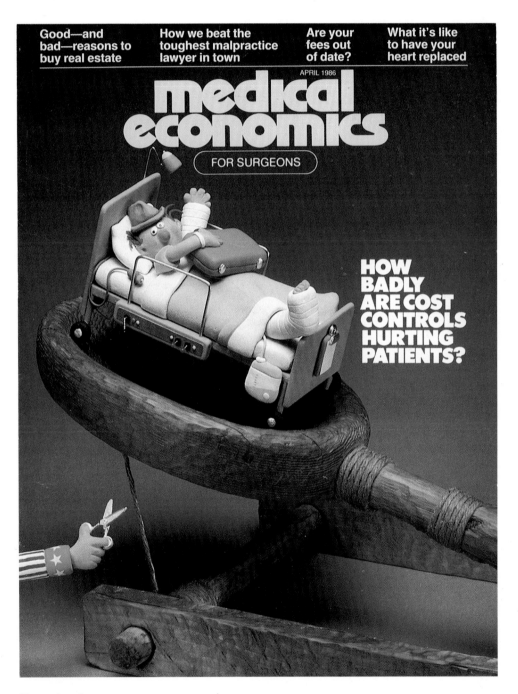

Dimensional
Illustrator: *Gordon Swenarton*
Art Director: *William Kuhn*
Photographer: *Stephen Munz*
Agency: *Medical Economics Company*
Publisher: *Jim Jenkins*
Client: *Medical Economics For Surgeons*
Category: *Editorial Magazine Business Cover*

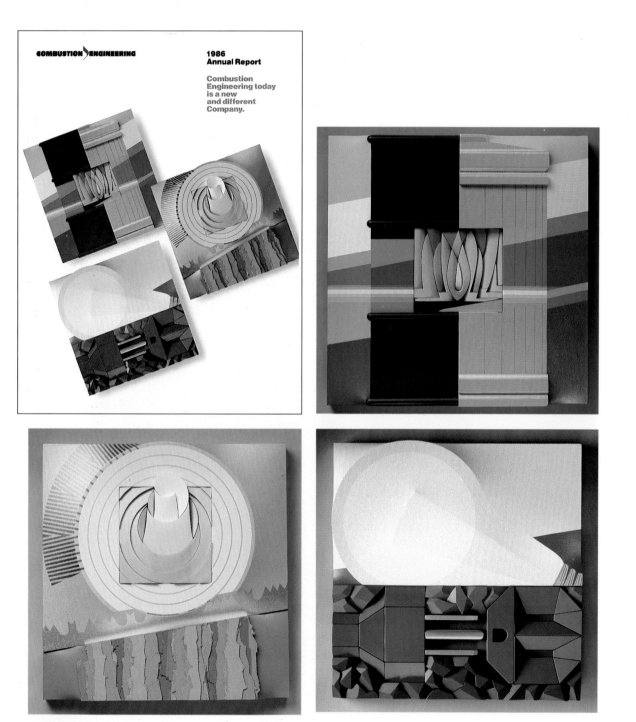

Dimensional
Illustrator: *Stephen Tarantal*
Art Director: *Jack Hough*
Photographer: *Dan Moerder*
Agency: *Jack Hough Associates*
Client: *Combustion Engineering*
Category: *Annual Report*

Dimensional
Illustrator: *Matthew Wurr*
Art Director: *David Stokes*
Photographer: *Graham Ford*
Agency: *Young & Rubicam*
Client: *Cinzano*
Category: *Magazine Advertising Spread*

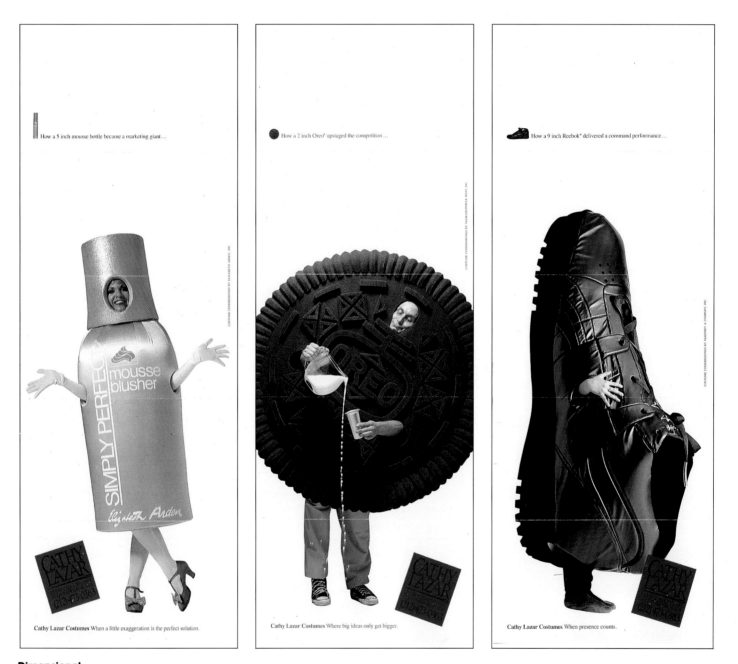

How a 5 inch mousse bottle became a marketing giant…

Cathy Lazar Costumes When a little exaggeration is the perfect solution.

How a 2 inch Oreo® upstaged the competition…

Cathy Lazar Costumes Where big ideas only get bigger.

How a 9 inch Reebok® delivered a command performance…

Cathy Lazar Costumes When presence counts.

Dimensional
Illustrator: *Cathy Lazar*
Art Director: *Barbara Nieminen*
Photographer: *Bob Murray*
Copy: *Cheryl Kaplan/McGrath/Power West,Inc*
Client: *Reebok/Elizabeth Arden/McKinsey*
Category: *Self Promotion*

184

Dimensional
Illustrator: *William Blahd*
Art Director: *Rob Sugar*
Photographer: *Tsantes Photography*
Agency: *Auras Design*
Client: *National Public Radio*
Category: *Advertising Direct Mail Poster*

SILVER
AWARD

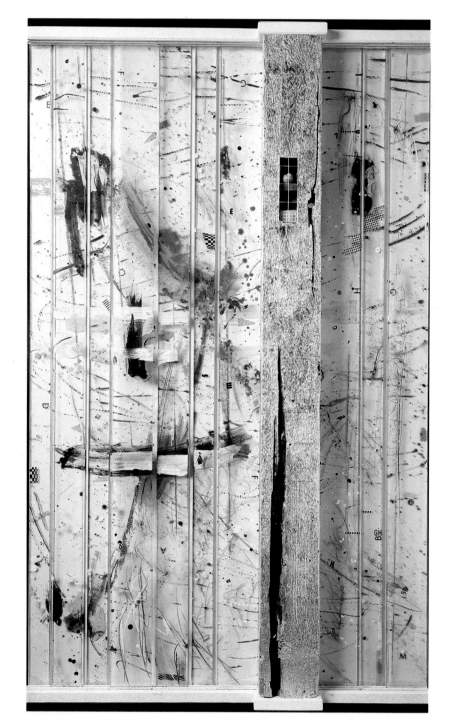

Dimensional
Illustrator: *Achim Kiel*
Art Director: *Achim Kiel*
Photographer: *Uwe Brandes*
Agency: *Pencil Corporate Art*
Publisher: *Pencil Art Editions*
Client: *Interpane Isolierglas West-Germany*
Category: *Editorial Illustration*

Dimensional
Illustrator: *Jerry Pavey*
Art Director: *Jerry Pavey*
Agency: *Jerry Pavey Design & Illustration*
Publisher: *Svec/Conway Printing and S & S Graphics, Inc.*
Client: *Farm Credit Banks Funding Corporation*
Category: *Editorial Illustration*

SILVER AWARD

Dimensional
Illustrators: *Asher & Lea Kalderon*
Art Director: *Asher Kalderon*
Photographer: *David Garb*
Agency: *Kalderon Studio*
Publisher: *Studio Arts*
Client: *Carmel Fruit Board of Israel*
Category: *Calendar*

Dimensional
Illustrator: *Christo*
Art Director: *Rudolph Hoglund*
Photographer: *Gianfranco Gorgoni*
Publisher: *Time Incorporated*
Category: *Magazine Editorial Consumer Cover*

M E R I T

A W A R D S

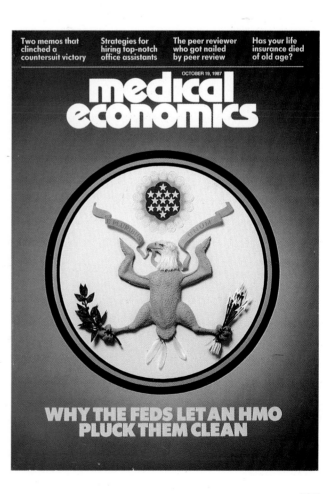

Dimensional
Illustrator: *Joan Steiner*
Art Director: *Roger Dowd*
Photographer: *Ken Schroers*
Agency: *Medical Economics Company*
Publisher: *Jim Jenkins*
Client: *Medical Economics Magazine*
Category: *Editorial Magazine Business Cover*

Dimensional
Illustrators: *Bass & Goldman*
Art Director: *Bill Johnson*
Photographer: *Marvin Goldman*
Agency: *Admarc*
Category: *Editorial Magazine Business Cover*

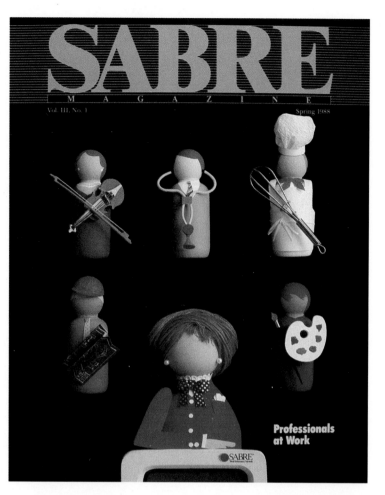

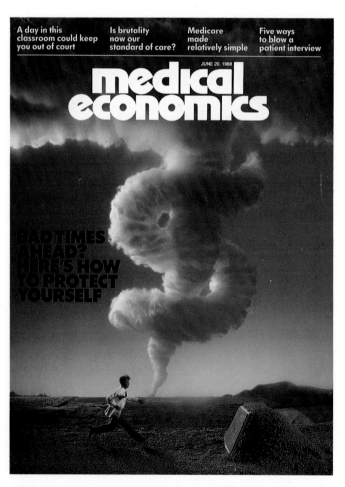

Dimensional
Illustrator: *Joan Steiner*
Art Director: *Roger Dowd*
Photographer: *Stephen Munz*
Agency: *Medical Economics Company*
Publisher: *Jim Jenkins*
Client: *Medical Economics Magazine*
Category: *Editorial Magazine Business Cover*

Dimensional
Illustrator: *Joan Steiner*
Art Director: *Roger Dowd*
Photographer: *Stephen Munz*
Agency: *Medical Economics Company*
Publisher: *Jim Jenkins*
Client: *Medical Economics Magazine*
Category: *Editorial Magazine Business Cover*

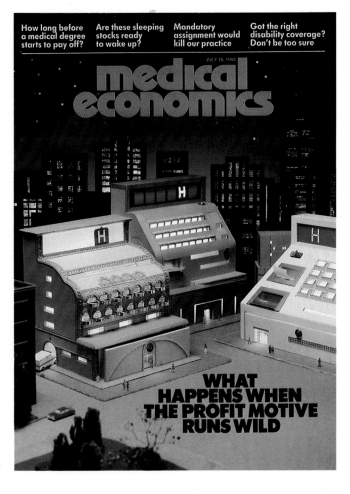

Dimensional
Illustrator: *Joan Steiner*
Art Director: *Roger Dowd*
Photographer: *Stephen Munz*
Agency: *Medical Economics Company*
Publisher: *Jim Jenkins*
Client: *Medical Economics Magazine*
Category: *Editorial Magazine Business Cover*

Dimensional
Illustrator: *James Nazz*
Art Director: *Frank Andrello*
Photographer: *James Nazz*
Publisher: *Wall Street Computer Review*
Category: *Magazine Editorial Consumer Cover*

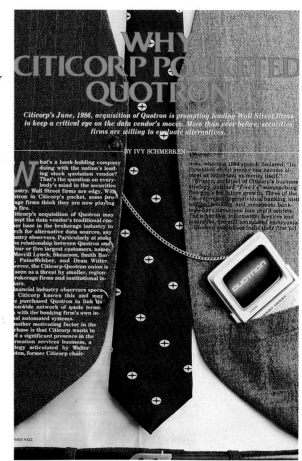

Dimensional
Illustrator: *Peter Angelo Simon*
Art Director: *Edward Rosanio*
Photographer: *Peter Angelo Simon*
Publisher: *Springhouse Corporation*
Client: *Nursing '88*
Category: *Magazine Editorial Business Spread*

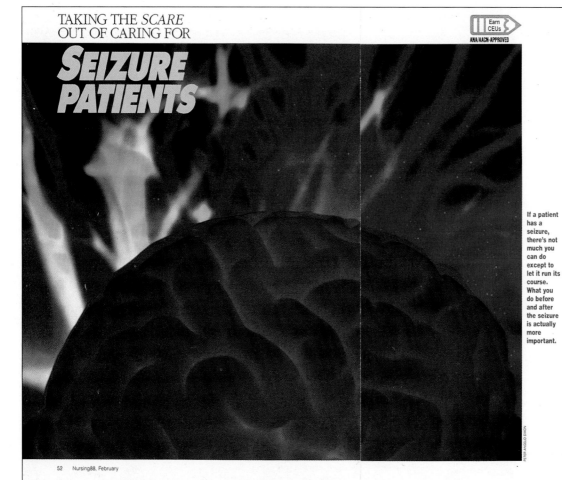

Dimensional
Illustrator: Frederick Walker
Art Director: Jake Smith
Photographer: Lynn Rosenthal
Publisher: Springhouse Corporation
Client: Learning '86
Category: Magazine Editorial Business Cover

Dimensional
Illustrator: Douglas Watson
Art Director: Douglas Watson
Photographer: Douglas McBride
Publisher: The Guardian Newspaper
Client: The Guardian
Category: Newspaper

Dimensional
Illustrator: *Robin Peterson*
Art Director: *Douglas Hunt*
Photographer: *Karl Steinbrenner*
Publisher: *New York Law Journal*
Client: *New York Law Journal*
Category: *Newspaper*

Dimensional
Illustrator: *Joe LaMantia*
Art Director: *Elizabeth Dodd*
Photographer: *Rodney Friend*
Publisher: *Indiana Review*
Client: *Indiana University Department of English*
Category: *Editorial Magazine Consumer Cover*

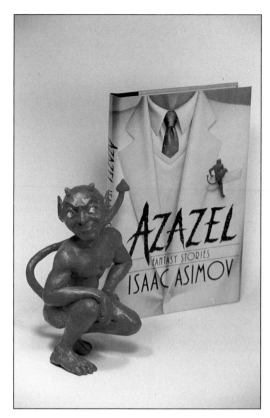

Dimensional
Illustrator: *Shaun Cusick*
Art Director: *Ken Pisani*
Photographer: *Shaun Cusick*
Publisher: *Doubleday Books*
Client: *Doubleday Books*
Category: *Book Cover*

Dimensional
Illustrator: *Joe LaMantia*
Art Director: *Elizabeth Dodd*
Photographer: *Chuck Burkhardt*
Publisher: *Indiana Review*
Client: *Indiana University Department of English*
Category: *Editorial Magazine Consumer Cover*

Dimensional
Illustrator: *Joe LaMantia*
Art Director: *Kim McKinney*
Photographer: *David Dudine*
Publisher: *Indiana Review*
Client: *Indiana University Department of English*
Category: *Editorial Magazine Consumer Cover*

Dimensional
Illustrator: *Joe LaMantia*
Art Director: *Elizabeth Dodd*
Photographer: *Ron Stout*
Publisher: *Indiana Review*
Client: *Indiana University Department of English*
Category: *Editorial Magazine Consumer Cover*
      Editorial Illustration

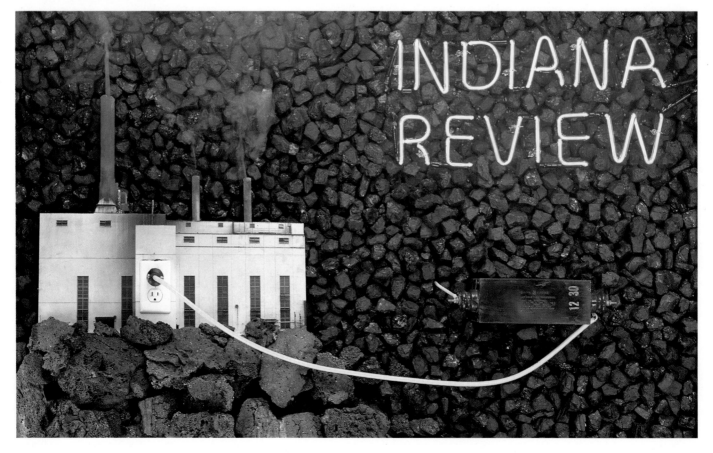

196

LOTTO JACKPOTS ARE NEVER CHICKEN FEED.

NEW YORK'S LOTTO 48

EVEN WHEN IT'S NOT WORTH ZILLIONS, IT'S WORTH MILLIONS.

Dimensional
Illustrator: *Cathy Lazar*
Art Director: *Mike Leon*
Photographer: *Jim Young*
Agency: *Rumrill Hoyt NY*
Client: *New York State Lottery*
Category: *Magazine Advertising Consumer*

LOTTO JACKPOTS ARE NEVER SMALL POTATOES.

NEW YORK'S LOTTO 48

EVEN WHEN IT'S NOT WORTH ZILLIONS, IT'S WORTH MILLIONS.

LOTTO JACKPOTS ARE NEVER JUST PEANUTS.

NEW YORK'S LOTTO 48

EVEN WHEN IT'S NOT WORTH ZILLIONS, IT'S WORTH MILLIONS.

Dimensional
Illustrator: *The Object Works*
Art Director: *George Titonis*
Photographer: *Tim Prendergast*
Agency: *Ketchum Advertising, Pittsburgh*
Client: *The Conair Group*
Category: *Magazine Advertising Business Spread*

A WORD OR TWO ABOUT THE NEXT HULA HOOP.*

Shake. Rattle. And Roll. That's what happens to the plastics industry when a phenomenon like the hula hoop hits. Everything moves. Materials, manpower, equipment. And, of course, millions of hips.

But if you wait for the next Frisbee; plastic car bumper, compact disc or PET bottle to hit, it may be too late. You have to start preparing your plastics processing operation as if the next job is... The Big One.

Introducing The Conair Group.

We're a select group of companies devoted specifically to meeting the needs of the plastics processing industry. Both now and in the future. At Conair, we design, build and install a full line of equipment and systems for heat transfer and robotic parts handling. We offer resin conveying and storage, polymer filtration, scrap reclaim, and size reduction equipment and systems. And we can do it all for you, anywhere in the world.

Conair also helps you plan for the equipment needs of your extrusion, injection molding, or blow molding operation. We offer turnkey auxiliary equipment systems, leasing, training, field service, and spares. And we deliver. On time. Guaranteed.

So get ready for a future of history-making ideas. With The Conair Group. For more information, call (800) 289-1289. Or write The Conair Group, 20 Stanwix Street, Pittsburgh, PA 15222.

Conair Franklin
Conair Jetro
Conair Churchill
Conair Pacific
Conair Martin
Conair Kawata
Conair Extrusion
Conair Leasing

We Guarantee Performance.

THE CONAIR GROUP

*Registered Trademark of WHAM-O.

Yesterday's DURACELL battery.

Today's DURACELL battery.

*F*OR A BRIGHTER HOLIDAY, USE TODAY'S DURACELL® BATTERIES.

Dimensional
Illustrator: *Michael Maniatis*
Art Director: *Rene Richmond*
Photographer: *Lynn Sugarman*
Agency: *Ogilvy & Mather*
Category: *Magazine Advertising Full Page*

Dimensional
Illustrator: *Mark Yurkiw Ltd. Staff*
Photographer: *Steve Bronstein*
Agency: *Calet, Hirsh, Spector*
Category: *Magazine Advertising Full Page*

Dimensional
Illustrator: *Christo Holloway*
Art Directors: *Chris Moss & Jon Rowley*
Photographer: *Adrian Flowers*
Agency: *Ted Bates Ltd.*
Client: *Benson & Hedges International*
Category: *Magazine Advertising Full Page*

Dimensional
Illustrator: *Michael Maniatis*
Art Director: *Rene Richmond*
Photographer: *Lynn Sugarman*
Agency: *Oglivy & Mather*
Category: *Magazine Advertising Spread*

THE MORAL OF TODAY'S STORY IS, USE DURACELL BATTERIES.

Dimensional
Illustrator: *Robin Peterson*
Art Director: *Richard Louie*
Photographer: *Michael Wilson*
Publisher: *Time Life*
Client: *People Magazine*
Category: *Advertising Business Brochure*

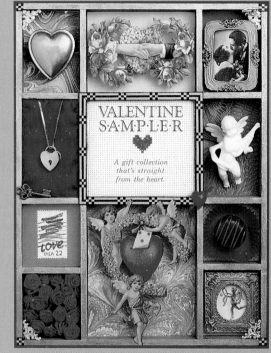

Dimensional
Illustrator: *Bob Emmott*
Art Directors: *Fred Yavorsky/Joe Caserta*
Photographer: *Bob Emmott*
Agency: *Ketchum Advertising, Philadelphia*
Client: *Dupont Electronics*
Category: *Magazine Advertising Business Spread*

If you want to increase the value of your PWB real estate, Du Pont can help you do it.

With VACREL* photopolymer film solder mask. The material that enables you to reliably encapsulate dense circuitry and tent via holes, permitting more electrical functions in less PWB real estate; to let you create higher density PWBs than ever before.

Instead of placing vias and components on separate areas of the board, you simply design vias under the components. And because VACREL tents the vias, solder stays only in the places where you want it; you avoid bridging, shorts, and contamination. It's also easier to clean under components.

In addition, you use less solder, minimizing assembly weight, because you're only covering connections. Hole-filling defects are also avoided. The bottom line is VACREL can increase assembly yields and cut manufacturing costs per function allowing you to get the most from your PWB real estate.

If you want more value out of your PWB real estate, ask for VACREL photopolymer film solder mask. It's the right material for PWB designs. Just call Du Pont at 1-800-237-4357. Or write: Du Pont Company, Room G-51176, Wilmington, DE 19898.

Du Pont Electronics
Share the power of our resources.

Dimensional
Illustrator: *Kathleen Ziegler*
Art Director: *Deborah Davis*
Photographer: *Kathleen Ziegler*
Agency: *LetterArts*
Copy: *Magge McCann*
Production Director: *Nick Greco*
Client: *Dimensional Illustrators, Inc.*
Category: *Advertising Direct Mail Business Poster*

Dimensional
Illustrator: *Thom M. Sandberg*
Art Director: *Thom M. Sandberg*
Photographer: *Mark Lafavor, Parallel Productions*
Agency: *The Kenyon Consortium*
Client: *Urban Wildlife*
Category: *Unpublished*

Dimensional
Illustrator: *Achim Kiel*
Art Director: *Achim Kiel*
Photographer: *Uwe Brandes*
Agency: *Pencil Corporate Art*
Publisher: *Pencil Art Editions*
Client: *Th. Kohl KG Apothekenbau W Germany*
Category: *Advertising Direct Mail Business*

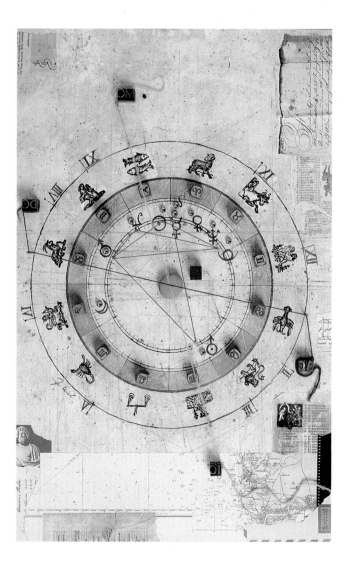

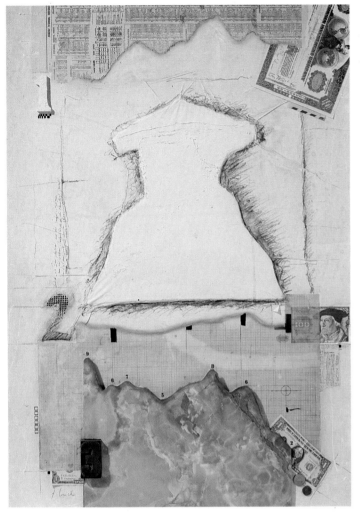

Dimensional
Illustrator: *Achim Kiel*
Art Director: *Achim Kiel*
Photographer: *Uwe Brandes*
Agency: *Pencil Corporate Art*
Publisher: *Pencil Art Editions*
Client: *Deutsche Genossenschafts-Hypothekenbank*
Category: *Advertising Direct Mail Business*

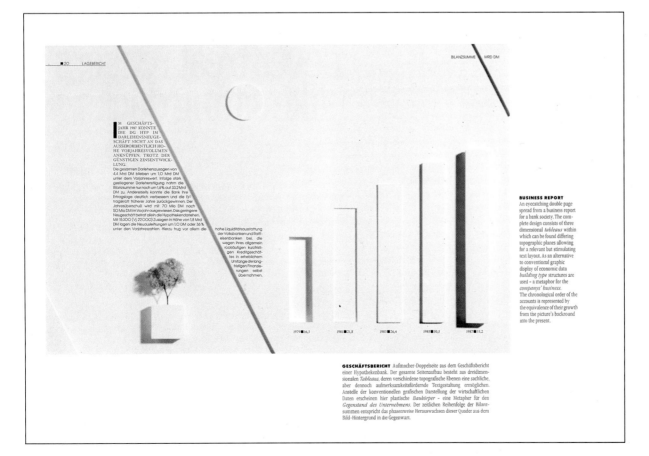

BUSINESS REPORT
An eyecatching double page
spread from a business report
for a bank society. The com-
plete design consists of three
dimensional *tableaus* within
which can be found differing
topographic planes allowing
for a relevant but stimulating
text layout. As an alternative
to conventional graphic
display of economic data
building type structures are
used – a metaphor for the
companys' business.
The chronological order of the
accounts is represented by
the equivalence of their growth
from the picture's background
into the present.

GESCHÄFTSBERICHT Aufmacher-Doppelseite aus dem Geschäftsbericht
einer Hypothekenbank. Der gesamte Seitenaufbau besteht aus dreidimen-
sionalen *Tableaus*, deren verschiedene topografische Ebenen eine sachliche,
aber dennoch aufmerksamkeitsfördernde Textgestaltung ermöglichen.
Anstelle der konventionellen grafischen Darstellung der wirtschaftlichen
Daten erscheinen hier plastische *Baukörper* – eine Metapher für den
Gegenstand des Unternehmens. Der zeitlichen Reihenfolge der Bilanz-
summen entspricht das phasenweise Herauswachsen dieser Quader aus dem
Bild-Hintergrund in die Gegenwart.

Dimensional
Illustrator: *James Nazz*
Art Director: *Orit Design*
Photographer: *Michael Tcherevkoff*
Agency: *Orit Design*
Publisher: *Sony Video*
Client: *Sony Video*
Category: *Video Cover*

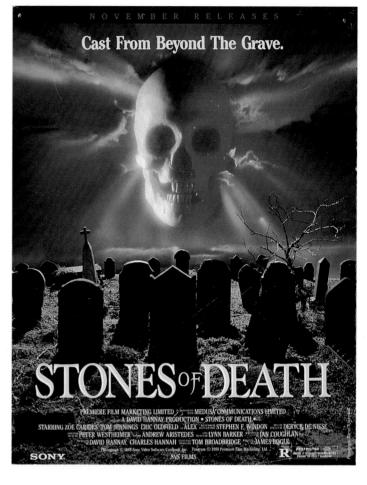

Dimensional
Illustrator: *Michael Maniatis*
Photographer: *Gary Feinstein*
Category: *Magazine Editorial Business Spread*

Our publications never treat readers like sitting ducks.

No two readers are identical. Each has unique needs, opinions and special interests.

In essence, there are no easy targets. And any magazine that treats readers like sitting ducks soon becomes a dead one.

That's why each McGraw-Hill magazine constantly works to remain vital and interesting to its audience. Each publication continuously evaluates itself. Readers are surveyed. Consultants are queried. Reportage is reviewed. Even the graphics are critiqued.

It's an expensive investment. It's also why our publications meet the ever-changing needs of our readers. We attract and keep their attention with informative, up-to-the-minute journalism.

McGraw-Hill publications deliver this editorial excellence with 33 magazines in 16 major industries. From architecture to aerospace, textiles to trucking, we provide unmatched industry coverage. And we reach the right readers in those markets. Owners. Presidents. Managers. Engineers. People who influence their industries. Decision-makers you want to influence.

Find out more about our well-read publications and the services McGraw-Hill offers you. Send for our free booklet, "The McGraw-Hill Advantage." Write Jack Sweger, Vice President-Marketing, McGraw-Hill Publications Company, 1221 Avenue of the Americas, New York, NY 10020.

McGraw-Hill Magazines
Your other sales force

Federal Home Loan Bank Board

1987 Annual Report

Dimensional
Illustrator: *Joan Hall*
Art Director: *Brian Walker*
Photographer: *Michael Pruzan*
Client: *Federal Home Loan Bank Board*
Category: *Annual Report*

Dimensional
Illustrator: *Bob Emmott*
Art Director: *Fred Yavorsky*
Photographer: *Bob Emmott*
Agency: *Ketchum Advertising Philadelphia*
Client: *Dupont Electronics*
Category: *Magazine Advertising Business Spread*

This little piggy went to market 5 months sooner thanks to Hybrid Circuits.

The faster you can make it, the faster you'll get your product to market. And in today's competitive climate, the best way to win your market is to get there first.

By using thick film hybrids as functional modules on printed boards, you can shrink a multilayer board to a double-sided board, cut costs by as much as thirty percent, and reduce design time from more than a year to a few months. It's that fast. It's that simple.

Thick-film material systems from DuPont give your high density circuits a competitive edge for virtually every electronic product.

Whatever you make, hybrid technology can make it smaller, faster, more reliably and economically. So while the competition stays home, you'll be laughing all the way to the bank.

Find out how hybrids can help get your products to market faster. Call **1-800-341-4004** for a free copy of our new brochure, "The future of Hybrids," or write: DuPont Company, Room G50959, Wilmington, DE 19898.

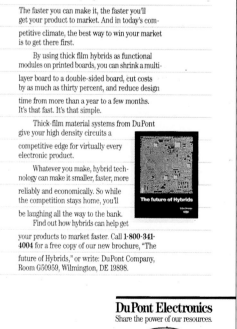

The future of Hybrids

DuPont Electronics
Share the power of our resources.

DUPONT

Dimensional
Illustrator: *Mark Yurkiw Ltd. Staff*
Art Director: *Bill Kopp*
Photographer: *Carl Zapp*
Agency: *McCann Erickson*
Client: *AT&T*
Category: *Advertising Illustration*

THE INTERPUBLIC GROUP OF COMPANIES, INC. ANNUAL REPORT 1988

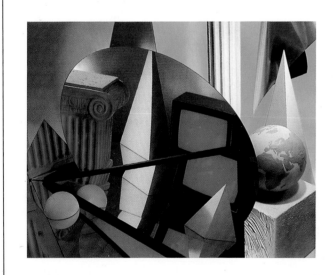

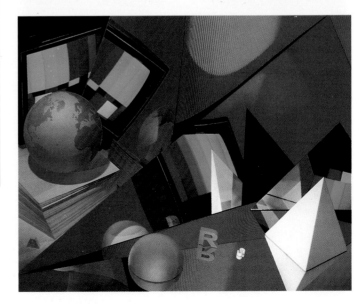

Dimensional
Illustrator: *Barbara Kasten*
Art Directors: *H.L. VanderBerg/E. Manasse*
Photographer: *Barbara Kasten*
Agency: *Lowe Marschalk/Pentagram Studio*
Client: *The Interpublic Group of Companies*
Category: *Annual Report*

Dimensional
Illustrators: *Carl Tese/Mark McAniff*
Art Director: *Seymour Chwast*
Photographer: *Marty Umans*
Agency: *Pushpin Graphics*
Category: *Unpublished*

Dimensional
Illustrator: *Prop Art McConnell & Borow, Inc.*
Art Director: *Kevin Donavan*
Photographer: *Cosimo*
Agency: *J. Walter Thompson*
Client: *Goodyear Tires*
Category: *Magazine Advertising Full Page*

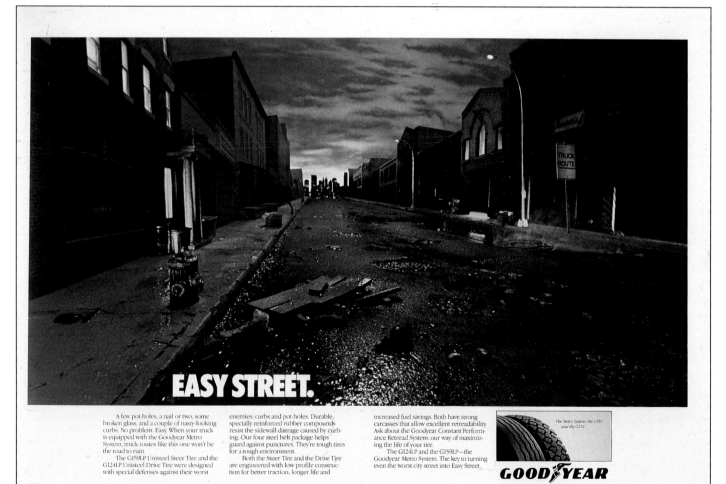

EASY STREET.

A few pot-holes, a nail or two, some broken glass, and a couple of nasty-looking curbs. No problem. Easy. When your truck is equipped with the Goodyear Metro System, truck routes like this one won't be the road to ruin.

The G159LP Unisteel Steer Tire and the G124LP Unisteel Drive Tire were designed with special defenses against their worst enemies: curbs and pot-holes. Durable, specially reinforced rubber compounds resist the sidewall damage caused by curbing. Our four steel belt package helps guard against punctures. They're tough tires for a tough environment.

Both the Steer Tire and the Drive Tire are engineered with low profile construction for better traction, longer life and increased fuel savings. Both have strong carcasses that allow excellent retreadability. Ask about the Goodyear Constant Performance Retread System: our way of maximizing the life of your tire.

The G124LP and the G159LP—the Goodyear Metro System. The key to turning even the worst city street into Easy Street.

The Metro System, the G159 and the G124

GOODYEAR

Dimensional
Illustrator: *James Nazz*
Art Director: *Ann Stevens*
Photographer: *James Nazz*
Publisher: *Psychology Today*
Category: *Illustration Editorial*

Dimensional
Illustrator: *Prop Art McConnell & Borow, Inc.*
Art Director: *Diana Cook-Tench*
Photographer: *Steve Bronstein*
Agency: *Morton Agency*
Client: *Alcatel Network Systems*
Category: *Magazine Advertising Full Page*

NOW YOUR REMOTE PHONE CUSTOMERS WON'T NOTICE A LITTLE PROBLEM AT THE CENTRAL OFFICE.

It's impossible to predict just what will disrupt phone service between your central office and your remote customers.

But, as sure as there are bad Japanese horror movies, one day something will.

Luckily, now there's a Digital Loop Carrier that will help you put your foot down and stamp out the problem once and for all. Introducing the Alcatel 300SA.

The 300SA is the only DLC that provides emergency stand-alone capability. So, no matter what disasters may strike the link with the main office, up to 240 of your customers will be able to keep on talking within their community.

But the 300SA is good for a lot more than emergencies; it's also an efficient substitute for a Remote Service Unit. It can be installed at between 50 and 75% of the cost, generate more income and fit nicely into your present telephone network.

If you'd like to know more about the Alcatel 300SA, just call 919-850-6000 or write to us at 3128 Smoketree Court, Raleigh, NC 27604.

ALCATEL
NETWORK SYSTEMS
©1987 Alcatel Corp

Dimensional
Illustrator: *The Object Works*
Art Director: *Larry Fredette*
Photographer: *Walt Seng*
Agency: *Beswick Communications*
Client: *AIM Automated Identification, Inc.*
Category: *Advertising Direct Mail Poster*

Dimensional
Illustrator: *Joan Steiner*
Art Director: *Sharon Rasmussen*
Photographer: *Walter Wick*
Agency: *Joan Steiner*
Publisher: *Whittle Communications*
Client: *Whittle Communications*
Category: *Editorial Illustration*

209

Dimensional
Illustrator: *James Nazz*
Art Director: *Bill Spencer*
Photographer: *James Nazz*
Publisher: *Time Magazine*
Category: *Illustration Editorial*

Dimensional
Illustrator: *Frank Miller*
Art Directors: *Hector Padron/Peter Zamiska*
Photographer: *Frank Miller*
Client: *ICI Pharma*
Category: *Advertising Magazine Business Spread*

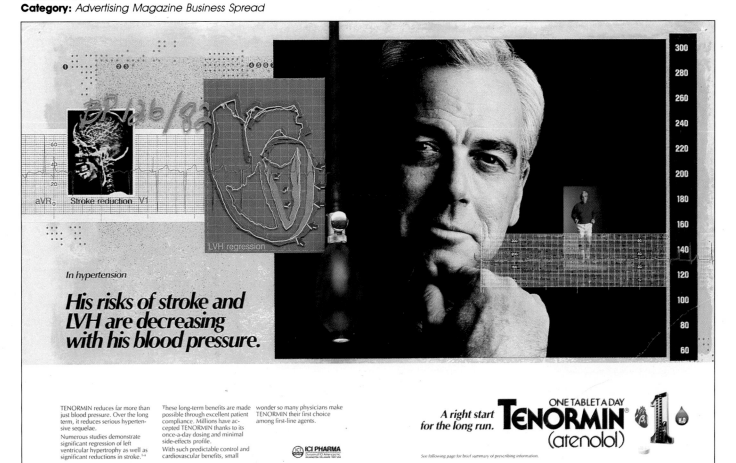

210

Dimensional
Illustrator: *Walter Einsel*
Art Director: *Roger Core*
Photographer: *Gordon Smith & Sons*
Client: *International Paper Company*
Category: *Advertising Illustration*

Dimensional
Illustrator: *Mark Yurkiw*
Art Director: *Yutaka Kawachi*
Photographer: *Yutaka Kawachi*
Category: *Advertising Illustration*

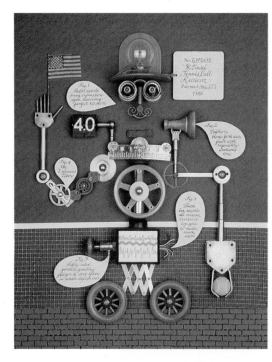

Dimensional
Illustrator: *Walter Einsel*
Art Director: *Kathy Burke*
Photographer: *Dom Furore*
Publisher: *New York Times*
Client: *Tennis Magazine*
Category: *Editorial Illustration*

Dimensional
Illustrator: *Peter Botsis*
Art Director: *Peter Botsis*
Photographer: *Sue Weller*
Agency: *Botsis Studios*
Publisher: *TSR Inc.*
Client: *Dragon Magazine*
Category: *Self Promotion Poster*

Dimensional
Illustrator: *Joan Hall*
Photographer: *Joan Hall*
Category: *Unpublished*

Dimensional
Illustrator: *Douglas Watson*
Art Director: *Douglas Watson*
Photographer: *Nick Price*
Category: *Editorial Illustration*

Dimensional
Illustrator: *Ellen Rixford*
Art Directors: *Susan Dinges/Sheila Sullivan*
Photographer: *Ellen Rixford*
Publishers: *Step-by-Step Graphics Magazine/People Magazine*
Clients: *Step-by-Step Graphics Magazine*
 People Magazine Promo Department
Category: *Editorial Illustration*

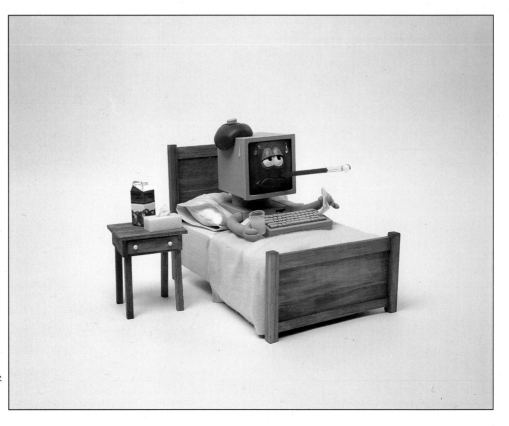

Dimensional
Illustrator: *Timothy Young*
Art Director: *Tom White*
Photographer: *John Carnett*
Publisher: *Times Mirror Magazines, Inc.*
Client: *Popular Science Magazine*
Category: *Editorial Illustration*

Dimensional
Illustrator: *Shaun Cusick*
Photographer: *Shaun Cusick*
Category: *Self Promotion*

Dimensional
Illustrator: *Tim Nyberg*
Art Director: *Tim Nyberg*
Photographer: *Eric Saulitis*
Agency: *Many Hats, Inc.*
Category: *Self Promotion*

Dimensional
Illustrator: *Eric Pervukhin*
Art Director: *Eric Pervukhin*
Photographer: *Eric Pervukhin*
Agency: *Pervukhin Studio*
Client: *Pervukhin Studio*
Category: *Editorial Illustration*

Dimensional
Illustrator: *James Nazz*
Art Director: *James Nazz*
Photographer: *James Nazz*
Category: *Self Promotion*

216

Dimensional
Illustrator: *Peter Buchman*
Photographer: *Peter Buchman*
Category: *Unpublished*

Dimensional
Illustrator: *Beth Gregerson*
Art Director: *Beth Gregerson*
Photographer: *Mike Wilkes*
Agency: *Luna Studio*
Category: *Unpublished*

Dimensional
Illustrator: *Kristin B. Moore*
Art Director: *Kristin B. Moore*
Photographer: *Mark W.A. Schreyer*
Agency: *Print/Bob Lopez, Potomac*
Clients: *Emily Hofstatter/Andrew Moore*
Category: *Unpublished*

Dimensional
Illustrator: *Joan Hall*
Photographer: *Joan Hall*
Category: *Unpublished*

Dimensional
Illustrator: *Shaun Cusick*
Photographer: *Shaun Cusick*
Category: *Unpublished*

Dimensional
Illustrator: *Brian Sinclair*
Art Director: *Dwight Harmon*
Photographer: *Michael Sean*
Category: *Unpublished*

Dimensional
Illustrator: *Mimi Foord*
Art Director: *Mimi Foord*
Photographer: *Keith Blohm Photography*
Agency: *Smaller Than Life Productions*
Category: *Unpublished*

Dimensional
Illustrator: *Jef Workman*
Art Director: *Jef Workman*
Photographer: *Mark Rice*
Agency: *PS Video Film Works*
Client: *PS Video Film Works*
Category: *Unpublished*

219

SINGULAR MEDIUMS

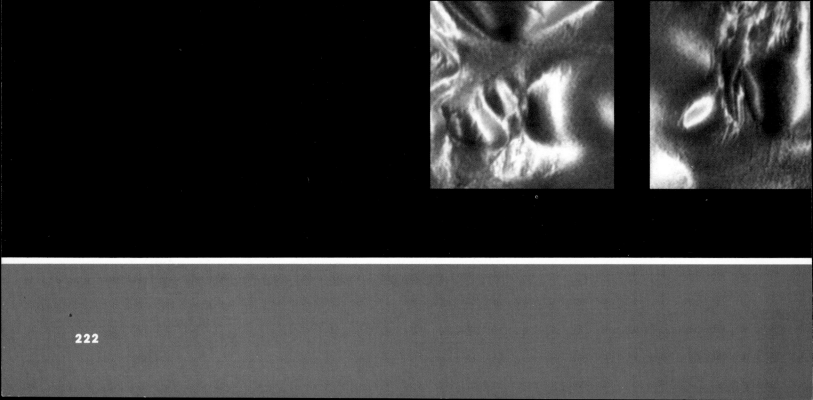

THE SINGULAR MEDIUM CATEGORY CONCEN-
TRATES PRIMARILY ON THE ILLUSTRATORS
ABILITIES TO WORK WITHIN A MEDIUM THAT IS
QUITE UNIQUE AND ALWAYS DEMANDING. THESE
MEDIUMS ENCOMPASS A WIDE RANGE OF
MATERIALS THAT CHALLENGE THE INGENUITY OF
THE ARTIST AND AWAKEN THE CURIOSITY OF THE
VIEWER. THE FOLLOWING CHAPTER INCLUDES
3-DIMENSIONAL MODELS FABRICATED FROM
METAL, PLASTER, GLASS, FOAM, SAND, EDIBLE
FOODS, WAX AND OTHER MATERIALS WHERE THE
OVERALL DIMENSIONAL ILLUSTRATION IS
PREDOMINANTLY THAT ONE MEDIUM.

SINGULAR MEDIUMS

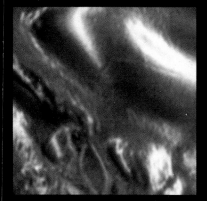

"Few mediums afford such life-like realism, such playful punnery and such conceptual artistry. And few graphic design fields require of its practicing artists such depth and breadth in such a wide variety of skills, methods and disciplines. Yet all too often the typical response a dimensional illustration will evoke from its awe struck viewers is: "Gee, is that a photo or an illustration? How did the artist actually create it? How long did it take them?" Surely, the First Annual Dimensional Illustrators Awards Show should do much to increase general awareness of this art form, as well as to advance the aesthetic appreciation of this exciting visual communications field."
NANCY ALDRICH-RUENZEL

FACIAL EXPRESSION

MARY QUANT
COSMETICS

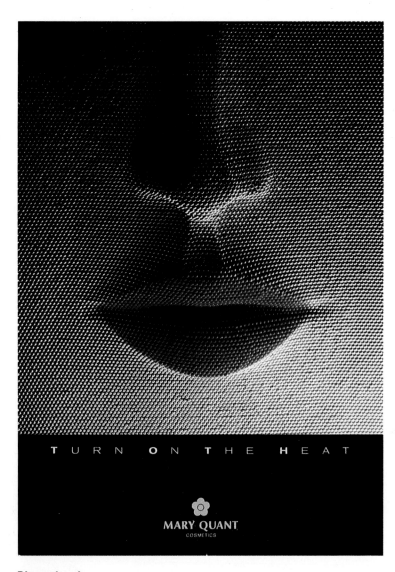

TURN ON THE HEAT

MARY QUANT
COSMETICS

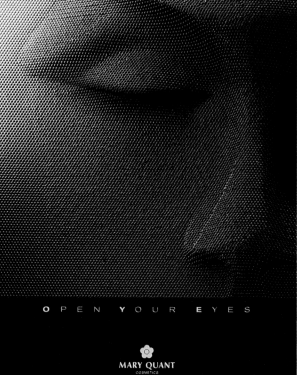

OPEN YOUR EYES

MARY QUANT
COSMETICS

Dimensional
Illustrator: *Matthew Wurr*
Art Director: *Peter Hobden*
Photographer: *Jerry Oke*
Agency: *Grey Advertising Ltd.*
Client: *Mary Quant Cosmetics*
Category: *Magazine Advertising Consumer Campaign*
Medium: *Metal*

Dimensional
Illustrator: Mark Yurkiw
Art Director: Bob Reitzfeld
Photographer: Robert Ammirati
Agency: Altschiller, Reitzfeld,
 Davis, Tracy-Locke
Category: Book Cover
Medium: Metal

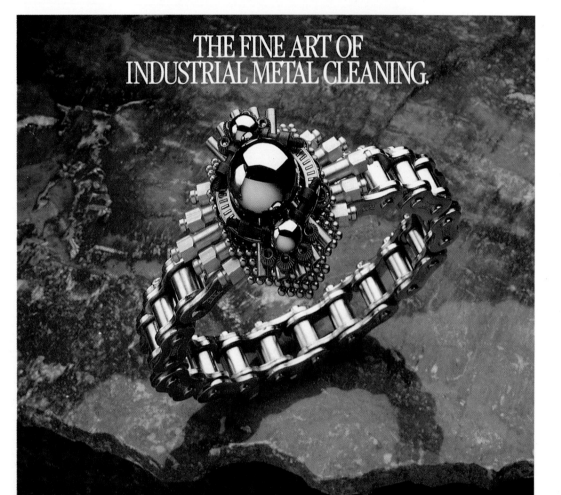

Dimensional
Illustrator: *Peter Sutherland*
Art Director: *Lynn Ridley*
Photographer: *Ray Boudreau*
Agency: *Kelley Advertising, Inc.*
Client: *Dow Chemical Canada, Inc.*
Category: *Advertising Illustration*
Advertising Magazine Campaign
Advertising Magazine Full Page
Medium: *Metal*

Dimensional
Illustrator: *Peter Sutherland*
Art Director: *Lynn Ridley*
Photographer: *Ray Boudreau*
Agency: *Kelley Advertising, Inc.*
Client: *Dow Chemical Canada, Inc.*
Category: *Advertising Magazine Full Page*
         Advertising Magazine Campaign
Medium: *Metal*

THE GOODS.
TIN MILL PRODUCTS FROM NATIONAL STEEL.

MAKING GOOD IN CANNED GOODS.

To make good in your business, you've got to deliver a quality product, of course. But you also have to get that product to market at the lowest possible price.

Steel, naturally, makes the lighter, thinner, stronger cans you demand. But you need more than just steel.

You need a packaging partner to share new ideas and new materials for the future.

National Steel is ready to work with you to help lower your costs, keep your container quality high, and help you make longer, smoother production runs.

We're ready to deliver the goods.

THE GOODS FROM NATIONAL STEEL.

We've concentrated tin mill production at our Midwest Division in Portage, Indiana. There, we produce a full line of tin mill products for every type of can you make—draw-redraw, drawn-and-ironed or three-piece cans.

Count on us for electrolytic tin plate, electrolytic chromium steel and black plate, in single—or double-reduced, all with the exact physical properties you need.

Dimensional
Illustrator: *The Object Works*
Art Director: *Wayne Boswell*
Photographer: *Chuck Bell*
Agency: *Burson/Marsteller, Inc.*
Client: *National Intergroup*
Category: *Advertising Direct Mail Business*
Medium: *Gelatin*

Dimensional
Illustrator: *Olive Alpert*
Art Director: *H. Bleiweiss*
Photographer: *Victor Scocozza*
Publisher: *Hearst*
Client: *Good Housekeeping*
Category: *Editorial Magazine Consumer Spread*
Medium: *Gingerbread*

A to Z.
We offer a single source for the urethane additives you need.

Right now, Air Products has a product line of over 100 pure and blended urethane additives. Additives like DABCO® crystal, DABCO 33-LV®, POLYCAT® 8, DABCO T-9, DABCO BL-11 and DABCO DMEA catalysts. Additives that are standards in every kind of urethane application from car seats to refrigerators, furniture to shoe soles.

And, of course, we're expanding our arsenal of LK® surfactants, AIRLIFT® mold release agents, and DABCO crosslinkers to maximize the effectiveness of your formulation.

The good part is that with all of our off-the-shelf products, chances are

we'll have a urethane additive to meet your need. Which is precisely what so many people who formulate polyurethanes have discovered, and why a number of our urethane additives are practically household words in the industry.

But, we don't stop there. For those customers with special needs, we offer an extensive custom design capability. During the past year we've introduced dozens of new products and conducted hundreds of trials throughout the world.

It's an enviable record no other urethane additives supplier can match.

So, if you need urethane expertise, start here. We can provide an additives package using commercial items, or a complete custom formulation. Air Products and Chemicals, Inc., Performance Chemicals Division, Box 538, Allentown, PA 18105. (800) 345-3148 (In PA, 215-481-6799). In Europe, 31-30-511828.
©Air Products and Chemicals, Inc., 1987

Call anytime.
Take advantage of our tech service in your urethane formulations.

We treat technical service as a full time job. Not just as a service used to help sell something. We're as near as your phone.

If you're working on a new urethane product, we can provide a lot of help at almost any point in the process by designing an additive specifically for your needs. We have an immense knowledge base for problem solving. Involving us in formulation design can be a cost-effective way to cut your product development costs.

Our ability to provide R&D

support and a broad range of existing products means you always get our best advice. Not the advice that's best for us. And our R&D capability keeps our tech service on the leading edge, and able to go the farthest to advance your product.

These capabilities developed the first delayed-action catalyst that was non-corrosive. And the first delayed-action catalyst that also shortened demolding times.

If you need a urethane catalyst or additive, give us a call. Get us

involved. We can do your product a lot of good, and help keep your formulating costs in check.
Air Products and Chemicals, Inc., Performance Chemicals Division, Allentown, PA 18195. 800-345-3148. Telex: 847416. In Europe, 31-30-511828.
©Air Products and Chemicals, Inc., 1987

When urethanes take a new direction, it's usually because we helped to find a new way to go.

Twenty-five years ago we set the polyurethane industry on its ear with the advent of Dabco® crystal catalyst — a new product that made the one-shot process possible. Revolutionary then. Standard procedure now.

Since then we've built a tradition more than 100 additives long, pointing the way in urethanes technology. We've married a substantial research and development commitment to the search for problem solving products. And it's paid off. For the whole urethanes industry.

We're still exploring in urethanes — with innovative products like Dabco SE catalyst used to delay cream times and accelerate curing in ethylene glycol-extended polyester

foams. Our Dabco HB catalyst does the same job in 1,4 butane-diol-extended foams. Both are making a big imprint in the shoe business.

Dabco TMR-4 catalyst is a rigid isocyanurate catalyst for pour-in-place systems—everything from entry doors to cooler panels. Currently, products like Dabco X-543 catalyst define the leading edge of additives technology, providing shortened demold and quick cure for your flexible molded foams. These advantages make it particularly useful in the auto industry.

We're committed to being important in urethane additives. Toward that end we've built a state-of-the-art technical lab in Allentown, and supported it with additional facilities in The

Netherlands and Japan.

Though needs change, our commitment to urethanes research doesn't. So, make it work for you. Get in touch and find out how much we can do to help your entire product development cycle.

Air Products and Chemicals, Inc., Performance Chemicals Division, Allentown, PA 18195. 800-345-3148. Telex: 847416. In Europe, 31-30-511828.
©Air Products and Chemicals, Inc., 1987

Dimensional
Illustrator: *Bob Emmott*
Art Director: *Doug Hill*
Photographer: *Bob Emmott*
Agency: *Lewis Gilman & Kynett*
Client: *Air Products & Chemicals*
Category: *Magazine Advertising Business Campaign*
Medium: *Urethane Foam*

SILVER
AWARD

Flying may have lost the elegance of the Twenties. Writing, however has regained it.

The moon shatters in some dark lagoon as the flying boat touches down.

Distracted by the faint tinkling that announces the arrival of your gin sling, you idly wonder, can it really be another 18 hours to Cairo?

Ah, the faded memories of a more romantic age.

The Parker Duofold was destined to remain just another of them. Until our centenary gave us the opportunity to recreate this sixty year old classic.

Like its predecessor, today's Duofold Centennial has a nib that is cut from a sheet of gold, and is, as always, slit by hand.

The casing too is produced exactly as it was in the Twenties, by machining from a solid block.

In only one respect does the Duofold Centennial depart from its forebear's specification. Inside, you will find the most advanced ink flow system ever designed: a series of tiny fins collect any surplus ink, ensuring an even flow.

The result is that today's Duofold can be expected never to leak. Even if you take it up in an aeroplane.

Which these days, may be the only way left to put some of the glamour back into flying.

◆ PARKER

Dimensional
Illustrator: *Matthew Wurr*
Art Director: *Dave Christensen*
Photographer: *Daniel Jouanneau*
Agency: *Lowe Howard Spink*
Client: *Parker Pens*
Category: *Magazine Advertising Spread*
Medium: *Metal*

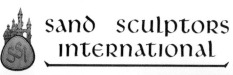

Dimensional
Illustrator: *Todd Vander Pluym & Staff*
Art Director: *Todd Vander Pluym*
Photographer: *Chad Slattery*
Category: *Self Promotion Brochure*
Medium: *Sand*

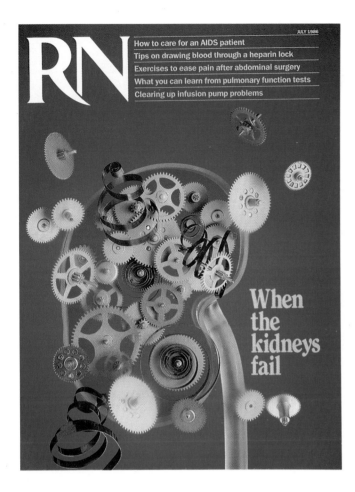

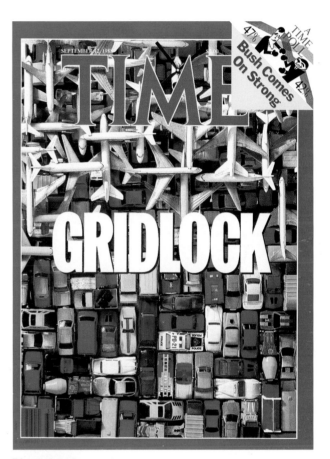

MERIT AWARDS

Dimensional
Illustrator: Bill Schmeelk
Art Director: Andrea DiBenedetto
Photographer: Stephen Munz
Agency: Medical Economics Company
Publisher: Lee Hufnagel
Client: RN Magazine
Category: Editorial Magazine Business Cover

Dimensional
Illustrator: Mirko Ilic
Art Director: Rudolph Hoglund
Photographer: Roberto Brosan
Publisher: Time Incorporated
Category: Magazine Editorial Consumer Cover
Medium: Metal

Dimensional
Illustrator: Bob Schuchman
Art Director: Tom Medsger
Photographer: Gary Moss
Publisher: MacMillan
Client: Respiratory Management
Category: Editorial Magazine Business Cover
Medium: Wax

Dimensional
Illustrator: *Olive Alpert*
Art Director: *H. Bleiweiss*
Photographer: *Victor Scocozza*
Publisher: *Hearst*
Client: *Good Housekeeping*
Category: *Editorial Magazine Consumer Cover*
Medium: *Gingerbread*

Dimensional
Illustrator: *Olive Alpert*
Art Director: *H. Bleiweiss*
Photographer: *Victor Scocozza*
Publisher: *Hearst*
Client: *Good Housekeeping Magazine*
Category: *Editorial Magazine Consumer Spread*
Medium: *Gingerbread*

"God bless the master of this house"—a New England saltbox authentic down to the slope of the roofline— "likewise the mistress too!" As you can see, the master is shaping the Yule log, the mistress, delivering gifts.

A whole street of little shops, from a toy store to a dress emporium— plus a bank to finance all the shopping! (For more winners, like this one, in our Gingerbread Contest, see page 16.)

Sixth Prize (one of 10): Main Street by Teresa Johnson, Warren, Conn.

234

Dimensional
Illustrator: *Olive Alpert*
Art Director: *H. Bleiweiss*
Photographer: *Victor Scocozza*
Publisher: *Hearst*
Client: *Good Housekeeping Magazine*
Category: *Editorial Magazine Consumer Cover*
Medium: *Gingerbread*

Gingerbread
Gallery

For the merriest of holidays, here is our brand-new collection of gingerbread houses. Make our fairy-tale cottage and the trio on the opposite page from our how-to's on page 216

Gingerbread designs: This page and opposite page, top, Olive Alpert, photographed by Victor Scocozza. Opposite page, bottom, design and photograph by Gene Machamer.

MORE ▶

Dimensional
Illustrator: *Olive Alpert*
Art Director: *H. Bleiweiss*
Photographer: *Victor Scocozza*
Publisher: *Hearst*
Client: *Good Housekeeping*
Category: *Editorial Magazine Consumer Spread*
Medium: *Gingerbread*

Dimensional
Illustrator: *Olive Alpert*
Art Director: *H. Bleiweiss*
Photographer: *Victor Scocozza*
Publisher: *Hearst*
Client: *Good Housekeeping*
Category: *Editorial Magazine Consumer Campaign*
Medium: *Gingerbread*

Dimensional
Illustrator: *Bob Schuchman*
Art Director: *Tom Medsger*
Photographer: *Gary Moss*
Publisher: *MacMillan*
Client: *Perinatology Neonatology*
Category: *Editorial Magazine Business Cover*
Medium: *Wax*

Dimensional
Illustrator: *The Object Works*
Art Director: *Caroline Fisher*
Photographer: *Joel De Grand*
Agency: *Ketchum Advertising, Pittsburgh*
Client: *Digital Equipment Corporation*
Category: *Magazine Advertising Business Spread*
Medium: *Plaster*

Dimensional
Illustrator: Brenda Pepper
Art Director: Becky Busching
Photographer: Peter Nicholas
Agency: Sieber & McIntyre
Client: Sandoz
Category: Advertising Direct Mail Consumer
Medium: Bread

For a
good day
and a
good night,
too

Once in
the morning,
once
at night

New
Tavist Syrup
(clemastine fumarate) 0.67 mg/5 ml

Allergy relief for kids...*
12 hours long

*Indicated for kids 6 years and older

Convenient
b.i.d. dosage
eliminates need to
take medication to
school

The low drowsi-
ness† antihistamine
now available in a
pleasant-tasting
liquid form

Rx only, so you
control your
patient's medication

LIVING ON BORROWED TIME.

A fire-scorched beam falls. Your buddy is trapped. The low-pressure alarm on his SCBA goes off and you realize that he will be out of air within minutes.

Quickly, without interrupting your air flow, you connect his regulator to yours with your emergency transfill air hose. Immediately, your buddy gets air as the transfilling between the two cylinders begins.

His pressure gauge begins to climb. Seconds later, the process is complete. You disconnect the hose and grab his arm reassuringly. You're just given him more time to breathe.

Introducing the Quick-Fill™ System from MSA. The first EEBSS (Emergency Escape Breathing Support System) that, when used, maintains NIOSH approval of the SCBA.

With the Quick Fill System, firefighters can now transfill air between SCBA cylinders. Even if one cylinder is high pressure and the other low pressure.

NIOSH-approved Quick Fill System allows fast emergency transfill between cylinders.

The Quick Fill System also gives you the convenience of compressor-to-SCBA or cascade system-to-SCBA filling capabilities, while still wearing your SCBA. A feature that saves time by eliminating cylinder changeover, while reducing the number of spare cylinders necessary.

Get the confidence of the Quick-Fill System from MSA. Because a little help between friends can go a long way toward saving lives. To arrange a demonstration, or to get more information, contact your local MSA fire service distributor. Or dial MSA's nearest branch office toll-free at 1-800-MSA-2222.

When it's MSA, you don't just wear it... You wear it with confidence.

MSA

Dimensional
Illustrator: The Object Works
Art Director: George Titonis
Photographer: Joel De Grand
Agency: Ketchum Advertising, Pittsburgh
Client: MSA (Mine Safety Appliances)
Category: Magazine Advertising Business Spread
Medium: Foam

Dimensional
Illustrator: Brenda Pepper
Art Director: Becky Busching
Photographer: Peter Nicholas
Agency: Sieber & McIntyre
Client: Sandoz
Category: Advertising Direct Mail Consumer
Medium: Bread

Dimensional
Illustrator: *Warren Lee Cohen*
Photographer: *Scott Stearns*
Category: *Unpublished*
Medium: *Bread*

Dimensional
Illustrator: *The Object Works*
Art Director: *Vince Longo*
Photographer: *Rudy Muller*
Agency: *Ketchum Advertising*
Client: *PNC Financial Corp*
Category: *Magazine Advertising Spread*
Medium: *Metal*

WHAT MAKES A NEW FINANCIAL CORPORATION MORE THAN JUST ANOTHER FINANCIAL CORPORATION.

A major factor is the quality of the merger. It is the precise blending of consistent management styles, complementary areas of expertise, and proven performance.

On January 19, Pittsburgh National Corporation and Provident National Corporation merged to form PNC Financial Corp, the 27th largest bank holding company in America.

These two institutions have demonstrated remarkable similarity in management – creative in approach, conservative in action. Yet each possesses a singular expertise that can benefit the other.

Both have been consistently profitable. Their returns on assets and equity have ranked both of them among the most profitable financial corporations in the country.

PNC Financial Corp: a merger of strength.

PNC FINANCIAL CORP

PNC Financial Corp, Pittsburgh, Pennsylvania
Subsidiaries: Pittsburgh National Bank • Provident National Bank •
The Kissell Company • Provident of Delaware Bank • PNC Discount Corp.
Nasdaq Symbol: PNCF

Dimensional
Illustrator: *Jerry Pavey*
Art Director: *Jerry Pavey*
Agency: *Jerry Pavey Design & Illustration*
Publisher: *Svec/Conway Printing and S & S Graphics, Inc.*
Client: *Farm Credit Banks Funding Corporation*
Category: *Editorial Illustration*
Medium: *Leather & Nails Construction*

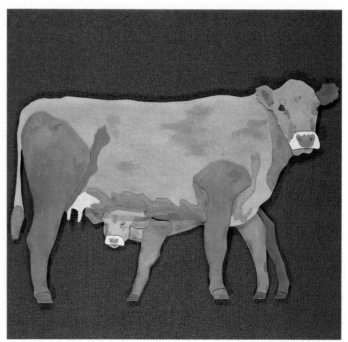

Dimensional
Illustrator: *Jerry Pavey*
Art Director: *Jerry Pavey*

Dimensional
Illustrator: *Bob Schuchman*
Art Director: *Bob Schuchman*
Photographer: *Bob Schuchman*
Category: *Unpublished*
Medium: *Plaster*

Dimensional
Illustrator: *Bob Schuchman*
Art Director: *Bob Schuchman*
Photographer: *Bob Schuchman*
Category: *Unpublished*
Medium: *Plaster*

Dimensional
Illustrator: *Matthew Wurr*
Art Director: *Karen Hagman*
Photographer: *Jerry Oke*
Agency: *Edwards Martin Thornton*
Client: *Tennent's Lager*
Category: *Magazine Advertising Spread*
Medium: *Aluminum Bas Relief*

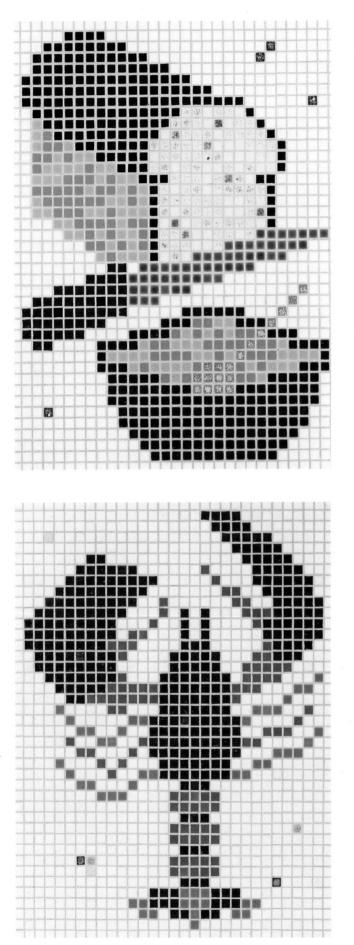

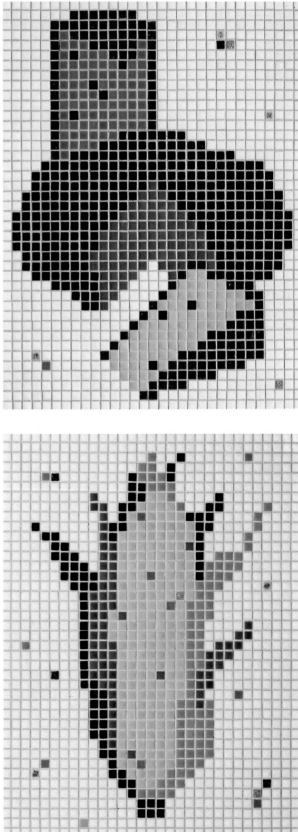

Dimensional
Illustrator: *Jerry Pavey*
Art Director: *Jerry Pavey*
Agency: *Jerry Pavey Design & Illustration*
Publisher: *Svec/Conway Printing and S & S Graphics, Inc.*
Client: *Farm Credit Banks Funding Corporation*
Category: *Editorial Illustration*
Medium: *Ceramic Tile Assemblage*

Dimensional
Illustrator: *Rosemary Littman*
Art Director: *Rosemary Littman*
Photographer: *Rosemary Littman*
Category: *Unpublished*
Medium: *Cake & Icing*

Dimensional
Illustrator: *Brenda Pepper*
Photographer: *Brenda Pepper*
Category: *Editorial Illustration*
Medium: *Bread*

advertising and publishing industries to the extended realities of 3-Dimensional Illustration. With your support we will continue to expand the use of dimensional illustration in the visual communications field and recognize today's gifted modelmakers for their sculptural expertise and creative 3-Dimensional artistry.

For further information or entry forms contact: Deadline for entries May 30, 1991.

Nick Greco
Dimensional Illustrators, Inc.
362 Second Street Pike, Suite 112
Southampton, PA 18966

Telephone: 215-953-1415
Fax: 215-953-1697

Dimensional Illustrators, Inc. was formed in 1985 by Kathleen Ziegler and Nick Greco with the express purpose of creating and promoting 3-Dimensional Illustrations in the advertising and publishing industry. An award winning design studio, they specialize in 3-Dimensional illustrations, models and props for the advertising, pharmaceutical, publishing and television industries. Models are created in all mediums including plastics, clay, acrylic, wood, paper and foam. Special effects photography is combined with dimensional models to produce conceptually stunning and visually stimulating 3-Dimensional illustrations.

They have created 3-Dimensional illustrations for publications including, Discover, Health, RN, Nursing '89, Learning, Medical Economics, Anesthesiology, Emergency Medicine, Drug Therapy, Diagnosis, and Geriatrics magazines. In addition, their work has appeared in advertisements and brochures for many of the nations leading pharmaceutical companies including, Smith Kline, Parke-Davis, Wallace Labs, and Rorer Pharmaceuticals.

Dimensional Illustrators, Inc. has received awards from the Association of Medical Illustrators Show, Desi Awards Show, RX Club Awards, and the Philadelphia Art Directors Awards Show. After successfully competing in numerous illustration award shows, they felt the need to produce an exhibition and competition that would recognize the accomplishments of the many talented 3-Dimensional illustrators and art directors who are creatively associated with the visual communications field. In 1989, The First Annual Dimensional Illustrators Awards Show was exhibited at the prestigious Art Directors Club of New York. The immense success of this show has resulted in the creation of, 3-Dimensional Illustration The Best In 3-D Advertising And Publishing Worldwide.

DIMENSIONAL ILLUSTRATORS, INC.

World Model
Kathleen Ziegler

THE FOLLOWING DIRECTORY OF 3-DIMENSIONAL

ILLUSTRATORS REPRESENTS THE WINNERS OF THE

FIRST ANNUAL DIMENSIONAL ILLUSTRATORS

AWARDS SHOW AND EXHIBITION. ENTRIES WERE

RECEIVED FROM THE UNITED STATES, ENGLAND,

SCOTLAND, DENMARK, HOLLAND, FRANCE,

ISRAEL, GERMANY, CHINA AND CANADA. ILLUS-

TRATORS ARE LISTED BY THE MEDIUMS IN WHICH

THEY SPECIALIZE.

DIRECTORY

Directory

Of

Dimensional

Illustrators

Worldwide

3 - D   M E D I C A L   I L L U S T R A T I O N

Ziegler, Kathleen
Dimensional Illustrators, Inc
362 2nd Street Pike / Suite 112
Southampton, PA 18966
215-953-1415

3 - D   P R O P S   &   S P E C I A L   E F F E C T S

Maniatis, Michael
Manhatten Model Makers
48 West 22nd Street
New York, NY 10010
212-620-0398

B R E A D   S C U L P T U R E

Cohen, Warren Lee
7904 Louise Lane
Wyndmore, PA 19118
215-242-0294

Pepper, Brenda
157 Clinton Street
Brooklyn, NY 11201
718-875-3236

C A K E   &   I C I N G

Littman, Rosemary
Rosemary's Cakes Inc.
299 Rutland Avenue
Teaneck, NJ 07666
201-833-2417

C E R A M I C   T I L E S   A S S E M B L A G E S

Pavey, Jerry
Jerry Pavey Design & Illustration
507 Orchard Way
Silver Spring, MD 20904
301-384-3377

C H O C O L A T E

Victor, Jim
272 High Street
Philadelphia, PA 19144
215-843-1327

C I G A R E T T E S

Victor, Jim
272 High Street
Philadelphia, PA 19144
215-843-1327

C L A Y   S C U L P T U R E

Arroyo, Andrea
Andrea Arroyo Studio
P.O. Box 1472
New York, NY 10009
212-477-2485 / Fax 212-979-5229

Bass, Marilyn
Marvin Bass & Goldman, Inc.
R.D. 3, Gypsy Trail Road
Carmel, NY 10512
914-225-8611

Botsis, Peter
Botsis Studio
2467 Culver Road
Rochester, NY 14609
716-544-1928

Carey, Sue
Sue Carey Illustration/Design
1700 Bush Street / #9
San Francisco, CA 94109
415-441-7046

Daniels, Shelley
1718 1/4 North Avenue/46
Los Angeles, CA 90041
213-257-9654

Foord, Mimi
Smaller Than Life Productions
1595 Stanford Street
Concord, CA 94519
415-680-0493

Graham, Jack
Graham Illustration
4415 E. Ashurst Drive
Phoenix, AZ 85044
602-759-9353

Gregerson,Beth
Luna Studio
35362 A. South Turtle Trail
Willoughby, OH 44094
216-975-0327

Jeffers, Kathy
151 West 19th Street, 3rd FL
New York, NY 10011
212-255-5196

Lallky, Bonnie J.
6600 NE 22nd Way, #2301
Fort Lauderdale, FL 33308
305-772-9734

Goldman, Marvin
Bass & Goldman, Inc.
R.D. 3 Gypsy Trail Road
Carmel, NY 10512
914-225-8611

McNeel, Richard
530 Valley Road, #2G
Upper Montclair, NJ 07043
201-509-2255

Nazz, James
159 2nd Avenue
New York, NY 10003
212-228-9713

Purcell, R. Scott
Parlor Productions
543 W. Rolling Road
Springfield, PA 19064
215-544-0874

Quick, Sheila
450 West 58th Street
New York, NY 10019
212-408-2118

Rixford, Ellen
Ellen Rixford Studio
308 West 97th Street, No.71
New York, NY 10025
212-865-5686

Rothman, Solomon
Rothman Studios
112 Elmwood Avenue
Bogota, NJ 07603
201-489-8833

Schuchman, Bob
5347 Linda Drive
Torrance, CA 90505
213-376-1448

Sievers,Lee
Sievers' Studio
5516 Queen Avenue So.
Minneapolis, MN 55410
612-929-1726

Swenarton, Gordon
Falcone & Associates
13 Watchung Avenue
Chatham, NJ 07928
201-635-2900

Jim Victor
272 High Street
Philadelphia, PA 19144
215-843-1327

Willard, Mike
2450 Mesquite Terrace
Olathe, KS 66061
913-782-5512

Workman, Jef
Bird In The Hand Studio
310 Carmel Avenue
Pacific Grove, CA 93950
408-372-9010

Young, Timothy
262 Waverly Avenue
Brooklyn, NY 11205
718-857-3283

Ziegler, Kathleen
Dimensional Illustrators, Inc
362 2nd Street Pike / Suite 112
Southampton, PA 18966
215-953-1415

D Y E D   L E A T H E R   &   N A I L S   C O N S T R U C T I O N

Pavey, Jerry
Jerry Pavey Design & Illustration
507 Orchard Way
Silver Spring, MD 20904
301-384-3377

FABRIC & STITCHERY COLLAGE

Alpert, Olive
Olive Alpert/Design
9511 Shore Road
Brooklyn, NY 11209
718-833-3092

Bono, Mary M.
3-Dimensional Illustration
288 Graham Avenue,
Brooklyn, NY 11211
718-387-3774

Cusack, Margaret
124 Hoyt Street
Brooklyn, NY 11217
718-237-0145

Glad, Deanna
Deanna Glad Illustration
P.O. Box 4432
San Pedro, CA 90731
213-831-6274

Golak, Elaine
3000 Ford Road
Bristol, PA
215-785-3368

Gregerson, Beth
Luna Studio
35362 A. South Turtle Trail
Willoughby, OH 44094
216-975-0327

Lallky, Bonnie J.
6600 NE 22nd Way, #2301
Fort Lauderdale, FL 33308
305-772-9734

Lazar, Cathy
Cathy Lazar Costumes & Soft Props
155 East 23rd Street
New York, NY 10010
212-473-0363

Lengyel, Kathy
2306 Jones Drive
Dunedin, FL 34698
813-734-1382

Morton Hubbard, Ann
Hubbard & Hubbard Design
815 N. 1st Avenue Suite #1
Phoenix, Arizona 85003
602-252-6463

Pavey, Jerry
Jerry Pavey Design & Illustration
507 Orchard Way
Silver Spring, MD 20904
301-384-3377

Potter D'Amato, Janet
Free Lance Illustrator
32 Bayberry Street
Bronxville, NY 10708
914-779-6264

Rixford, Ellen
Ellen Rixford Studio
308 West 97th Street, No.71
New York, NY 10025
212-865-5686

B A S   R E L I E F   S C U L P T U R E   F A B R I C

Glad, Deanna
Deanna Glad Illustration
P.O. Box 4432
San Pedro, CA 90731
213-831-6274

C O S T U M E S

Lazar, Cathy
Cathy Lazar Costumes & Soft Props
155 East 23rd Street
New York, NY 10010
212-473-0363

FOAM SCULPTURE COSTUMES

Lazar, Cathy
Cathy Lazar Costumes & Soft Props
155 East 23rd Street
New York, NY 10010
212-473-0363

FRUIT

Victor, Jim
272 High Street
Philadelphia, PA 19144
215-843-1327

GINGERBREAD

Alpert, Oive
Olive Alpert/Design
9511 Shore Road
Brooklyn, NY 11209
718-833-3092

MEDICAL MODELS FOR COURTROOM DISPLAY

Schuchman, Bob
5347 Linda Drive
Torrance, CA 90505
213-376-1448

MEMORABILIA

Moore, Kristin B.
Lotas, Minard, Patton, McIver, Inc.
110 East 59th Street/28thFL
New York, NY 10022
212-486-3370 / 696-0593

METAL SCULPTURE

Pavey, Jerry
Jerry Pavey Design & Illustration
507 Orchard Way
Silver Spring, MD 20904
301-384-3377

MINIATURE SETS

Nazz, James
159 2nd Avenue
New York, NY 10003
212-228-9713

MIXED MEDIA ASSEMBLAGE

Hall, Joan
155 Bank Street / H954
New York, NY 10014
212-243-6059

Peterson, Robin
411 West End Avenue
New York, NY 10024
212-724-3479

MIXED MEDIA CONSTRUCTIONS

Pavey, Jerry
Jerry Pavey Design & Illustration
507 Orchard Way
Silver Spring, MD 20904
301-384-3377

MIXED MEDIA

Alpert, Olive
Olive Alpert/Design
9511 Shore Road
Brooklyn, NY 11209
718-833-3092

Arroyo, Andrea
Andrea Arroyo Studio
P.O. Box 1472
New York, NY 10009
212-477-2485 Fax 212-979-5229

Marilyn Bass
Bass & Goldman, Inc.
R.D. 3, Gypsy Trail Road
Carmel, NY 10512
914-225-8611

Blahd, William
3717 Alton Place N.W.
Washington, D.C. 20016
202-686-0179

Blauers, Nancy
50 Walnut Street
Stratford, CT 06497
203-377-6109

Borow, Mark
Prop Art/McConnell & Borow, Inc.
210 Elizabeth Street/2nd Floor
New York, NY 10012
212-941-9550

Botsis, Peter
Botsis Studio
2467 Culver Road
Rochester, NY 14609
716-544-1928

Buchman, Peter
517 East 77th Street, Apt. 3-1
New York, NY 10021
212-628-6956

Coleman, Mary Lynn
2903 W. 50 Terrace
Shawnee Mission, KS 66205
815-274-8033

Crawford, Wilbur
Crawford Design
90 Bethel Road
Glen Mills, PA 19342
215-358-3974/215-238-9000

Cusick, Shaun
Illustrator
2436 Maple Avenue
Seaford, NY 11783
516-781-1995

Einsel, Walter
26 Morningside Drive South
Westport, CT 06880
203-226-0709

Emmott, Bob
Emmott Studio, Inc.
700 South 10th Street
Philadelphia, PA 19147
215-925-2773

Foord, Mimi
Smaller Than Life Productions
1595 Stanford Street
Concord, CA 94519
415-680-0493

Gregerson, Beth
Luna Studio
35362 A. South Turtle Trail
Willoughby, OH 44094
216-975-0327

Hall, Joan
155 Bank Street / H954
New York, NY 10014
212-243-6059

Holloway, Christo
Mark Yurkiw Ltd.
568 Broadway/Suite 605
New York, NY 10012
212-226-6338

Ilic, Mirko
548 Hudson Street
New York, NY 10014

Kasten, Barbara
251 West 19th Street
New York, NY 10011

Kritchman/Knuteson Joan
Advertising Art Studios, Inc.
710 N Plankinton Avenue
Milwaukee, WI 53203
414-276-6306/FAX 414-276-7425

LaMantia, Joe
LaMantia Studio
820 W. Howe Street
Bloomington, IN 47401
812-332-2667

Lang, Cecily
250 East Royal Palm Road/1A
Boca Raton, FL 33432
407-392-5860

Lazar, Cathy
Cathy Lazar Costumes & Soft Props
155 East 23rd Street
New York, NY 10010
212-473-0363

Maniatis, Michael
Manhatten Model Makers
48 West 22nd Street
New York, NY 10010
212-620-0398

Marvin Goldman
Bass & Goldman, Inc.
R.D. 3, Gypsy Trail Road
Carmel, NY 10512
914-225-8611

Moore, Kristin B.
Lotas, Minard, Patton, McIver, Inc.
110 East 59th Street/28th FL
New York, NY 10022
212-486-3370/ 696-0593

Nazz, James
159 2nd. Avenue
New York, NY 10003
212-228-9713

Nyberg, Tim
Many Hats, Inc.
1012 Trillium Lane
P.O. Box 686
Sister Bay, WI 54234
414-854-4464

Otnes, Fred
26 Chalburn Road
West Redding, CT 06896
203-938-2829

Pavey, Jerry
Jerry Pavey Design & Illustration
507 Orchard Way
Silver Spring, MD 20904
301-384-3377

Pervukhin, Eric
Pervukhin Studio
2027 Burlison Drive
Urbana, IL 61801
217-399-3645

Peterson, Robin
411 West End Avenue
New York, NY 10024
212-724-3479

Rixford, Ellen
Ellen Rixford Studio
308 West 97th Street, No.71
New York, NY 10025
212-865-5686

Rothman, Solomon
Rothman Studios
112 Elmwood Avenue
Bogota, NJ 07603
201-489-8833

Sandberg, Thom
The Kenyon Consortium
#505 1221 Nicollet Mall
Minneapolis, MN 55403
621-332-8132

Schmeelk, Bill
Wellington Enterprises
55 Railroad Avenue, Bldg. 5
Garnerville, NY 10923
914-429-3377

Schuchman, Bob
5347 Linda Drive
Torrance, CA 90505
213-376-1448

Seman, Ronald
The Object Works
12 Eighth Street
Pittsburgh, PA 15222
412-261-3513

Simon, Peter Angelo
568 Broadway, Suite 701
New York, NY 10012
212-925-0890

Sinclair, Brian
S. 2203 Grand Boulevard
Spokane, WA 99206
509-747-8041

Sornat, Czeslaw
Czeslaw Sornat Illustration & Graphics
4521 Sidereal
Austin, TX 78727
512-836-9528

Steiner, Joan
Bate Road, Box 292, R.D. 1
Craryville, NY 12521
518-851-7199

Tarantal, Stephen
7923 Park Avenue
Elkins Park, PA 19117
215-635-3967

Victor, Jim
272 High Street
Philadelphia, PA 19144
215-843-1327

Workman, Jef
Bird In The Hand Studio
310 Carmel Avenue
Pacific Grove, CA 93950
408-372-9010

Young, Timothy
262 Waverly Avenue
Brooklyn, NY 11205
718-857-3283

Yurkiw, Mark
Mark Yurkiw Ltd.
568 Broadway, Suite 605
New York, NY 10012
212-226-6338

Ziegler, Kathleen
Dimensional Illustrators, Inc
362 2nd Street Pike / Suite 112
Southampton, PA 18966
215-953-1415

M O D E L   M A K I N G

Alpert, Olive
Oive Alpert Design
9511 Shore Road
Brooklyn, NY 11209
718-833-3092

Bass, Marilyn
Bass & Goldman, Inc.
R.D. 3, Gypsy Trail Road
Carmel, NY 10512
912-225-8611

Bono, Mary
3-Dimensional Illustration
288 Graham Avenue
Brooklyn, NY 11211
718-387-3774

Borow, Mark
Prop Art
210 Elizabeth Street/2nd FL
New York, NY 10012
212-941-9550

Buchman, Peter
517 East 77th Street, Apt. 3-1
New York, NY 10021
212-628-6956

Cusick, Shaun
Illustrator
2436 Maple Avenue
Seaford, NY 11783
516-781-1995

Einsel, Walter
26 Morningside Drive South
Westport, CT 06880
203-226-0709

Emmott, Bob
Emmott Studio Inc.
700 South 10th Street
Philadelphia, PA 19147
215-925-2773

Holloway, Christo
Mark Yurkiw Ltd.
568 Broadway, Suite 605
New York, NY 10012
212-226-6338

Kritchman / Knuteson, Joan
Advertising Art Studios, Inc.
710 N Plankinton Avenue
Milwaukee, WI 53203
414-276-6306 / FAX 414-276-7425

Maniatis, Michael
Manhatten Model Makers
48 West 22nd Street
New York, NY 10010
212-620-0398

Goldman, Marvin
Bass & Goldman, Inc.
R.D. 3, Gypsy Trail Road
Carmel, NY 10512
914-225-8611

Nazz, James
159 2nd Avenue
New York, NY 10003
212-228-9713

Schmeelk, Bill
Wellington Enterprises
55 Railroad Avenue, Bldg. 5
Garnerville, NY 10923
914-429-3377

Schuchman, Bob
5347 Linda Drive
Torrance, CA 90505
213-376-1448

Seman, Ronald
The Object Works
12 Eighth Street
Pittsburgh, PA 15222
412-261-3513

Sornat, Czeslaw
Czeslaw Sornat Illustration & Graphics
4521 Sidereal
Austin, TX 78727
512-836-9528

Steiner, Joan
Bate Road, Box 292, R.D. 1
Craryville, NY 12521
518-851-7199

Young, Timothy
262 Waverly Avenue
Brooklyn, NY 11205
718-857-3283

Yurkiw, Mark
Mark Yurkiw Ltd.
568 Broadway, Suite 605
New York, NY 10012
212-226-6338

Ziegler, Kathleen
Dimensional Illustrators, Inc
362 2nd Street Pike / Suite 112
Southampton, PA 18966
215-953-1415

P A P E R   C O L L A G E

Alpert, Olive
Olive Alpert/Design
9511 Shore Road
Brooklyn, NY 11209
718-833-3092

Ash, Susan
Ravenhill / Artist's Representative
PO Box 36364
Kansas City, MO 64111
913-677-0028 / FAX 913-677-0080

Bass, Marilyn
Bass & Goldman, Inc.
R.D. 3, Gypsy Trail Rd.
Carmel, NY 10512
914-225-8611

Baum, Susan
123 Palisade Street / #6
Dobbs Ferry, NY 10522
914-693-5143

Glaser, Milton
Milton Glaser, Inc.
207 East 32nd. Street
New York, NY 10016
212-889-3161

Hall, Joan
155 Bank Street / H954
New York, NY 10014
212-243-6059

Lang, Cecily
250 East Royal Palm Road / 1A
Boca Raton, FL 33432
407-392-5860

Goldman, Marvin
Bass & Goldman, Inc.
R.D. 3, Gypsy Trail Rd.
Carmel, NY 10512
914-225-8611

Norby, Carol H.
112 South Main
Alpine, Utah 84004
801-756-1096

Peterson, Robin
411 West End Avenue
New York, NY 10024
212-724-3479

Potter D'Amato, Janet
Free Lance Illustrator
32 Bayberry Street
Bronxville, NY 10708
914-779-6264

Uram, Lauren
Artist
251 Washington Avenue #4R
Brooklyn, NY 11205
718-789-7717

Yankus, Marc
570 Hudson Street Apt.3
New York, NY 10014
212-242-6334

P A P E R   P O P - U P S

Hatch, Wally
Intervisual Communications
Plains Road / P.O. 666
Essex, CT 06426

Ives, William
Ives Designs
7930 Barnes Street /Apt. B-4
Philadelphia, PA 19111
215-742-9947

Richwine, Jim
Structural Graphics
6151 West Century Bvld. Suite 400
Los Angeles, CA 90045

Scalera, Tomm
Tomm Scalera Graphics
87 First Avenue / Apt. 1B
New York, NY 10003
212-529-1817
(Pop-Up Cartoons)

Sornat,Czeslaw
Czeslaw Sornat Illustration & Graphics
4521 Sidereal
Austin, TX 78727
512-836-9528

P A P E R   S C U L P T U R E

Ajin
C/O Raymond Stringer
463 W 47th Street/Suite 2
New York, NY 10036
212-333-7377

Alavezos, Gus
2215 Ptarmigan Lane
Colorado Springs, CO 80918
719-528-6821

Alpert, Olive
Olive Alpert/Design
9511 Shore Road
Brooklyn, NY 11209
718-833-3092

Ash, Susan
Ravenhill / Artist's Representative
PO Box 36364
Kansas City, MO 64111
913-677-0028 / FAX 913-677-0080

Bandle, Johnna
JB Illustration
4502 Francis
Kansas City, KA 66103
913-722-0687

Bass, Marilyn
Bass & Goldman, Inc.
R.D. 3, Gypsy Trail Rd.
Carmel, NY 10512
914-225-8611

Cowan, Bob
528 Shelton Drive
Aberdeen, NC 28315
919-944-1306

Crawford, Wilbur
Crawford Design
90 Bethel Road
Glen Mills, PA 19342
215-358-3974

Crowe, Mark
Crowe Graphics
40032 Short Ridge Ct.
Oakhurst, CA 93644
209-683-4466

DeCerchio, Joseph
JDC Designs
62 Marlborough Avenue
Marlton, NJ 08053
609-596-0598

Finewood, Bill
Art Works Inc.
605 S Main Street
East Rochester, NY 14445
716-377-3126

Gregerson, Beth
Luna Studio
35362 A. South Turtle Trail
Willoughby, OH 44094
216-975-0327

Jackson, Bob
816 Bainbridge Street
Philadelphia, PA 19147
215-627-8413

Jordan, R.E.
5411 NE Circle Drive
Kansas City, MO 64119
816-453-5315

Kritchman /Knuteson, Joan
Advertising Art Studios, Inc.
710 N. Plankinton Avenue
Milwaukee, WI 53203
414-276-6306
FAX 414-276-7425

Lose, Hal
Toad Hall Graphics
533 W. Hortter Street
Philadelphia, PA 19119
215-849-7635

Marvin Goldman
Bass & Goldman, Inc.
R.D. 3, Gypsy Trail Rd.
Carmel, NY 10512
914-225-8611

Metzger, Angela
N.M. Barnum & Associates
117 South Charles
Belleville, IL 62220
618-234-6800

Miller, Bill
Bill Miller/Illustration
Suite 2002 D
1355 North Sandburg Terrace
Chicago, IL 60610
312-787-4093

Monahan, Leo
721 South Victory Boulevard
Burbank, CA 91502-2426
818-843-6115/818-842-8866

Nishinaka Jeff
362 North Crescent Hts Blvd.
Los Angeles, CA 90048

Nitzberg, Andrew
2101 Green Street
Philadelphia, PA 19130
215-765-8871

Nyberg, Tim
Many Hats, Inc.
P.O. Box 686
1012 Trillium Lane
Sister Bay, WI 54234
414-854-4464

Pavey, Jerry
Jerry Pavey Design & Illustration
507 Orchard Way
Silver Spring, MD 20904
301-384-3377

Potter D'Amato, Janet
Free Lance Illustrator
32 Bayberry Street
Bronxville, NY 10708
914-779-6264

Rixford Ellen
Ellen Rixford Studio
308 West 97th Street, No.71
New York, NY 10025
212-865 5686

Rothman, Solomon
Rothman Studios
112 Elmwood Avenue
Bogota, Rothman NJ 07603
201-489-8833

Schmitz, Paul
2108 NW 58 Street
Kansas City, MO 64151

Shein, Bob
15 Glenfield Lane,
Nesconset, NY 11767
516-265-0064

Trachsel Hanson, Mary
224 Loraine Avenue #2
Cincinnati, Ohio 45220
513-961-3348

Tysko, Lisa
Three-Six-One Design Group
361 Nassau Street
Princeton, NJ 08540
609-921-3610

Williams, Toby
Toby Williams Illustration
84 Franklin Street
Watertown, MA 02172
617-924-2406

Workman, Jef
Bird In The Hand Studio
310 Carmel Avenue
Pacific Grove, CA 93950
408-372-9010

PLASTIC SCULPTURE

Alpert, Olive
Olive Alpert/Design
9511 Shore Road
Brooklyn, NY 11209
718-833-3092

Aristovulos, Nick
16 East 30th Street
New York, NY 10016
212-725-2454

Arroyo, Andrea
Andrea Arroyo Studio
P.O. Box 1472
New York, NY 10009
212-477-2485
Fax 212-979-5229

Bass,Marilyn
Bass & Goldman, Inc.
R.D. 3, Gypsy Trail Road
Carmel, NY 10512
914-225-8611

Bono, Mary
3-Dimensional Illustration
288 Graham Avenue
Brooklyn, NY 11211
718-387-3774

Emmott, Bob
Emmott Studio, Inc.
700 South 10th Street
Philadelphia, PA 19147
215-925-2773

Holloway, Christo
Mark Yurkiw Ltd.
568 Broadway, Suite 605
New York, NY 10012
212-226-6338

Maniatis, Michael
Manhatten Model Makers
48 West 22nd Street
New York, NY 10010
212-620-0398

Marvin Goldman
Bass & Goldman, Inc.
R.D. 3, Gypsy Trail Road
Carmel, NY 10512
914-225-8611

Nazz, James
159 2nd. Avenue
New York, NY 10003
212-228-9713

Rixford, Ellen
Ellen Rixford Studio
308 West 97th Street, No.71
New York, NY 10025
212-865-5686

Schmeelk, Bill
Wellington Enterprises
55 Railroad Avenue, Bldg. 5
Garnerville, NY 10923
914-429-3377

Seman, Ronald
The Object Works
12 Eighth Street
Pittsburgh, PA 15222
412-261-3513

Young, Timothy
262 Waverly Avenue
Brooklyn, NY 11205
718-857-3283

Yurkiw, Mark
Mark Yurkiw Ltd.
568 Broadway, Suite 605
New York, NY 10012
212-226-6338

Ziegler, Kathleen
Dimensional Illustrators, Inc
362 2nd Street Pike/Suite 112
Southampton, PA 18966
215-953-1415
FAX 215-953-1697

PLASTER

Rixford, Ellen
Ellen Rixford Studio
308 West 97th Street, No.71
New York, NY 10025
212-865-5686

Schuchman, Bob
5347 Linda Drive
Torrance, CA 90505
213-376-1448

Victor, Jim
272 High Street
Philadelphia, PA 19144
215-843-1327

PHOTOGRAPHY

Emmott, Bob
Emmott Studio Inc.
700 South 10th Street
Philadelphia, PA 19147
215-925-2773

Simon, Peter Angelo
568 Broadway, Suite 701
New York, NY 10012
212-925-0890

PHOTO ILLUSTRATION

Bernstein, Audrey
33 Bleeker Street – 6A
New York, NY 10012
212-353-3512

SAND SCULPTURE

Vander Pluym, Todd
Sand Sculptors International
425 Via Anita
Redondo Beach, CA 90277
213-372-4250

SET DESIGN

Emmott, Bob
Emmott Studio Inc.
700 South 10th Street
Philadelphia, PA 19147
215-925-2773

S O F T   S C U L P T U R E   C H A R A C A T U R E S

Potter D'Amato, Janet
Free Lance Illustrator
32 Bayberry Street
Bronxville, NY 10708
914-779-6264

W A X   S C U L P T U R E

Schuchman, Bob
5347 Linda Drive
Torrance, CA 90505
213-376-1448

W O O D   &   M E T A L   A S S E M B L A G E S

Pavey, Jerry
Jerry Pavey Design & Illustration
507 Orchard Way
Silver Spring, MD 20904
301-384-3377

W O O D   S C U L P T U R E

Alpert, Olive
Olive Alpert/Design
9511 Shore Road
Brooklyn, NY 11209
718-833-3092

Arroyo, Andrea
Andrea Arroyo Studio
P.O. Box 1472
New York, NY 10009
212-477-2485
Fax 212-979 5229

Bass, Marilyn
Bass & Goldman, Inc.
R.D. 3 / Gypsy Trail Road
Carmel, NY 10512
914-225-8611

Blauers, Nancy
50 Walnut Street
Stratford, CT 06497
203-377-6109

Buchman, Peter
517 East 77th Street/Apt. 3-1
New York, NY 10021
212-628-6956

Coleman, Mary Lynn
2903 W. 50 Terrace
Shawnee Mission, KS 66205
815-274-8033

Einsel, Walter
26 Morningside Drive South
Westport, CT 06880
203-226-0709

Glad, Deanna
Deanna Glad Illustration
P.O. Box 4432
San Pedro, CA 90731
213-831-6274

Holloway, Christo
Mark Yurkiw Ltd.
568 Broadway/Suite 605
New York, NY 10012
212-226-6338

Maniatis, Michael
Manhatten Model Makers
48 West 22nd Street
New York, NY 10010
212-620-0398

Goldman, Marvin
Bass & Goldman, Inc.
R.D. 3 / Gypsy Trail Road
Carmel, NY 10512
914-225-8611

Nazz, James
159 2nd Avenue
New York, NY 10003
212-228-9713

Pavey, Jerry
Jerry Pavey Design & Illustration
507 Orchard Way
Silver Spring, MD 20904
301-384-3377

Rasmussen, Bonnie
A.Art/ B. Rasmussen Ltd.
8828 Pendleton
St. Louis, MO 63144
314-962-1842

Rixford, Ellen
Ellen Rixford Studio
308 West 97th Street, No.71
New York, NY 10025
212-865-5686

Rothman, Solomon
Rothman Studios
112 Elmwood Avenue
Bogota, NJ 07603
201-489-8833

Schmeelk, Bill
Wellington Enterprises
55 Railroad Avenue, Bldg. 5
Garnerville, NY 10923
914-429-3377

Sornat, Czeslaw
Czeslaw Sornat Illustration & Graphics
4521 Sidereal
Austin, TX 78727
512-836-9528

Victor, Jim
272 High Street
Philadelphia, PA 19144
215-843-1327

CLAY SCULPTURE

Chatwin, Robert
Plasticine Illustrator
25 Winnett Avenue
Toronto, Ontario
Canada M6G 3L2
416-657-8133

Watson, Douglas
2 Leadervale Road
Liberton
Edinburgh EH166PA
Scotland UK
031-6642524

FABRIC

Elsom, Vickey
3D Productions
95 Lawton Bvld / #607
Toronto, Ontario Canada M4V 128
416-489-6453

Kalderon, Asher
Kalderon Studio
P.O. Box 24070
Tel Aviv, Israel 69701
03-478281

FRUIT

Kalderon, Asher
Kalderon Studio
P.O. Box 24070
Tel Aviv Israel 69701
03 478281

METAL SCULPTURE

Kalderon, Asher
Kalderon Studio
P.O. Box 24070
Tel Aviv Israel 69701
03 478281

Kiel, Achim
Pencil Corporate Art
Heinrich-Buessing-Hof D-3300
Braunschweig, West Germany
0531-72964 / 72692

Sutherland, Peter
Peter Sutherland & Associates
276 Carlaw Avenue / Suite 201
Toronto, Ontario
Canada M4M 2S8
416-533-3917

Wurr, Matthew
Matthew Wurr Associates
Faith House
38 Kingsland Road
12 Perseverance Works
London, England E2 8DD
01 739 6666

MIXED MEDIA

Kalderon, Asher
Kalderon Studio P.O. Box 24070
Tel Aviv, Israel 69701
03-478281

Kiel, Achim
Pencil Corporate Art
Heinrich-Buessing-Hof
D-3300
Braunschweig West Germany
0531-72964 / 72692

Nagy, Peter
196 Lawrence Avenue West
Toronto, Ontario
Canada, M5M 1A8
416-487-8216

Watson, Douglas
2 Leadervale Road
Liberton
Edinburgh EH166PA
Scotland, UK
031-6642524

Wurr, Matthew
Matthew Wurr Associates
38 Kingsland Road
Faith House 12 Perseverance Works
London, England E2 8DD
01-739-6666
Fax 01-729-3838

PAPER SCULPTURE

Kalderon, Asher
Kalderon Studio
P.O. Box 24070
Tel Aviv, Israel 69701
03-478281

Chan, Edward S.F.
45 Orchard Park Blvd.
Toronto, Ontario
Canada M4L 3E3
416-698-6802

Thaae, Soren
3-D Illustrations
38 Auroravej
DK-2610 Copenhagen, Denmark
45 31 41 14 11

Tosetto, Jacques
Rue de Tre
Ervy Le Chatel, France
25 70 54 76

van Koppen, Josje
van Koppen
Statenweg 104 A
Rotterdam the Netherlands Holland
010-4676662

PLASTIC SCULPTURE

Kalderon, Asher
Kalderon Studio
P.O. Box 24070
Tel Aviv, Israel 69701
03-478281

PRECIOUS METALS

Wurr, Matthew
Matthew Wurr Associates
Faith House
38 Kingsland Road
12 Perseverance Works
London, England E2 8DD
01 739 6666

WOOD SCULPTURE

Wurr, Matthew
Matthew Wurr Associates
Faith House/12 Perseverance Works
38 Kingsland Road
London, England E2 8DD
01-739-6666

COLOR HARMONY

A step-by-step guide to choosing and combining colors, **Color Harmony** includes 1,662 individual color combinations; dozens of full-color photos to show you how your color schemes will look; a four-color conversion chart; 61 full-size charts and much more.

158 pages ISBN 0-935603-06-9
$15.95 Softcover

COLOR SOURCEBOOK I

Originally published with great success in Japan, **Color Sourcebook I** is a treasure trove of ideas for producing intriguing color combinations, shapes and patterns. Color concepts under the headings "Natural," "Oriental" and "High Tech" provide many interesting and useful color combinations to help create an appropriate color framework. Instructions are specific, geared toward the professional, yet clear enough to be useful to the student.

112 pages ISBN 0-935603-28-X
$15.95 Softcover

COLOR SOURCEBOOK II

Companion to **Color Sourcebook I**, this volume furnishes the designer with color concepts under the headings "Pop," "RetroModern" and "Post Modern."

112 pages ISBN 0-935603-29
$15.95 Softcover

GRAPHIC IDEA NOTEBOOK

The new revised softcover edition of this workhorse book contains 24 all-new pages. This book is a study in graphic design, covering innovative problem-solving, demonstrating techniques to turn routine material into provocative editorial presentation.

216 pages ISBN 0-935603-6406
$18.95 Softcover

CLICK

by J. Ellen Gerken

This first annual publication is devoted to "cutting edge" computer artwork. Included are commentaries on designs as well as a short "toolbox" listing the hardware and software used and the artist's or designer's name.

160 pages ISBN 0-89134-348-2
$39.95 Hardcover

HOT AIR

by Werner Steuer

The first in the Hot Air annual presentation of outstanding art will help keep artists, designers and their clients informed of the latest innovations and new creations in this dynamic art form. Instructional and aesthetic points are included.

176 pages ISBN 0-89134-345-8
$39.95 Hardcover

THE BEST OF AD CAMPAIGNS!

by Steve Blount & Lisa Walker

Get a behind-the-scenes look at the creation of more than 30 of the best recent international, national and local advertising campaigns, including California Raisin Advisory Board, Chevrolet, Diet Coke, Isuzu, Michelob, Pepsi-Cola and Visa USA. One-on-one interviews with the marketing directors of leading corporations and their ad agencies reveal how each campaign was conceived, the marketing strategy behind the advertising and why the campaign works.

256 pages ISBN 0-935603-09-3
$49.95 Hardcover

noAH III
DIRECTORY OF INTERNATIONAL PACKAGE DESIGN

Covering the best new work of over 70 top ranked package design studios from more than 20 countries, **noAH** is a stunning and comprehensive collection of the most unique and visually exciting corporate and brand packaging concepts. More than 1,000 full-color photographs are accompanied by essays on each firm's philosophy, history and operations strategies. Contains a list of addresses and telephone and fax numbers.

464 pages ISBN 4-931154-13-1
$89.95 Hardcover

TYPE & COLOR:
A Handbook of Creative Combinations

Graphic artists must perform quickly, creatively and accurately. **Type & Color** enables graphic artists to spec type in color quickly and efficiently. Ten sheets of color type styles printed on acetate overlays can be combined with hundreds of color bars, making it possible to experiment with thousands of color/type combinations right at the drawing board. In minutes, your eye will rapidly judge what the mind had conceived. 160 pages plus 10 pages of acetate overlays.

160 pages ISBN 0-935603-19-0
$34.95 Hardcover

SCREEN PRINTING DESIGN

by Lisa Walker & Steve Blount

A showcase for excellence in graphics of all types, **Screen Printing Design** is the first book devoted exclusively to silk screened works. More than 400 photos represent the best current screen printed work of graphic designers, illustrators, artists and screen printers worldwide, both in visual design and technique.

240 pages ISBN 0-935603-17-4
$49.95 Hardcover

Volume One:
TRADEMARKS & SYMBOLS OF THE WORLD: THE ALPHABET IN DESIGN

This wonderful idea book presents more than 1,700 contemporary designs for every letter of the alphabet. An essential resource for anyone who designs logos and corporate identities.

192 pages ISBN 4-7601-0451-8
$24.95 Softcover

Volume Two:
TRADEMARKS & SYMBOLS OF THE WORLD: DESIGN ELEMENTS

If you design packages, ads, corporate logos or signage, you must have this resource guide in your design library. It features more than 1,700 design elements that can add pizzazz to any printed piece.

192 pages ISBN 4-7601-0450-X
$24.95 Softcover

Volume Three:
PICTOGRAM & SIGN DESIGN

This book is packed with 1,800 pictogram and sign designs from all over the world. They were selected for their unique ability to nonverbally convey a message: no left turn, clothes must be worn here, flammable, camel crossing, beware, volcanic activity, eclairs available, I Love You - and 1793 more.

232 pages ISBN 0-935603-30-1
$24.95 Softcover

LETTERHEAD & LOGO DESIGNS
Creating the Corporate Image

by Steve Blount & Lisa Walker

A recognizable and effective visual identity is a necessity for businesses of all sizes and types, from makers of consumer goods to restaurants and retail stores. **Letterhead & Logo Designs** is a comprehensive selection of the most exciting and effective current designs for corporate identity packages, including letterheads, business cards, envelopes, stationery supplies, logotypes and more.

256 pages ISBN 0-935603-37-9
$49.95 Hardcover

The Best New U.S. & International
LABEL DESIGNS 2

by Steve Blount & Lisa Walker

Seven chapters are devoted to major categories of label and package design: foods, snacks, beverages, consumer goods, health & beauty aids, wines, beer & liquor, cosmetics, media products, and clothing. Included is the best recent work of leading graphic design firms including The Duffy Design Group, Harte Yamashita & Forest, and Primo Angeli Inc.

256 pages ISBN 0-935603-31-X
$49.95 Hardcover